Leave 'Em in the Dust

Build With the Nazarene Carpenter

Written by Jim Douglas

This book is a work of non-fiction. Unless otherwise noted, the author and the publisher make no explicit guarantees as to the accuracy of the information contained in this book.

Most Scripture quotations are taken from the King James Version of the Bible. Some are from The Holy Bible, English Standard Version® (ESV®), copyright © 2001 by Crossway, a publishing ministry of Good News Publishers. Used by permission. All rights reserved.

Because of the dynamic nature of the Internet, any web addresses or links contained in this book may have changed since publication and may no longer be valid. The views expressed in this work are solely those of the author.

Endorsements for Leave 'Em in the Dust

I have known Jim Douglas for over two decades and was marked by his commitment to biblical manhood and womanhood; values that our contemporary society seems to be progressively watering down. His ministry approach in pouring out his life into some of us has not only transformed ministry for us, but also enabled us to return to the Great Commission following Jesus' mandate of making disciples. I know the heart of the matter is the matter of the heart. What's on God's heart? Make disciples of all nations.

Bro.Joe Jikong, Ph.D. APC, Pastor, Etugebe Baptist Church, Yaounde Cameroon

"Leave 'Em in the Dust" is an all-hands-on-deck work of a man who has faithfully invested about a quarter century of his life into intentional, strategic disciple making on several continents. It is a must read for anyone with a worldwide vision and passion for making disciples."

Njini Edward Lemnga, Pastor, Nkewn Baptist Church, Bamenda Cameroon

For more than ten years Jim Douglas has been discipling me, annually in person, in China. For the past two years he has been discipling me, and a small group that I lead, through WeChat and Zoom. As a result of his investment in me, disciple making has become the engine of my life. Jim has lived this teaching before my eyes. I and my wife, Helen, have adopted Jim as our Dad. Our two daughters know him only as Ye-Ya (Chinese for Grandpa), and he honored us by naming our number one daughter, Abby. For the past several years I have traveled to more than 25 Chinese Provinces, to many churches, teaching the truths of disciple making just as it has

4

been taught to me. We are seeing multiplying disciples through this ministry in a wonderful way. The teachings in this book have changed and given power to my Christian life, and given me God's vision. You will become what you behold. But you will not become what you can't see. You will be like what you strongly look at. My Dad, Jim, has helped me to see and become someone who can see! God's direct command to me, and all believers, is to make disciples of all nations. As the result of this teaching, the Lord has given me grace to disciple churches in China, Shri Lanka, Chenai India, and the Philippine Islands. May this book help open the eyes of your heart and help you to see and see more!

Brian Feng, Discipler, Beijing China and the world

For many years I've read books on discipleship. Each fervently identifies the importance of making disciples. Some even go as far as to give a programmatic approach to the discipleship concept. The book in your hands is different. Jim's approach to the Christian life is steeped in discipling others in the truth trusted to him, the one true God revealed in Scripture. You will see in these pages truth to be shared with reliable men, who then share with others. Perhaps you too, have read many books on discipleship, and they left you feeling like a failure. Read this - you'll find it a refreshing reminder (maybe a first reminder) that disciple making is rooted in passing on the truth trusted to you. Then go, do it. Jim has documented a framework for you to follow.

John Weathersby, Pastor

First Reformed Baptist Church, Harrisburg, PA

I have had the pleasure of being able to work with Jim over the past few years and I've experienced first-hand, not only his drive for disciple making, but also his love for Christ and for God's people. This book is not theory, but is the result of worldwide 'boots on the ground' disciple making. Anchored in scripture, this is a volume that provides valuable material to live into the Great Commission. I am certain that all who read it will be enriched and encouraged.

John Nickolas, Pastor/Director Adult Education

First Reformed Baptist Church, Harrisburg, Pa

Dedication

This book is dedicated to help equip the Christian Saints by exposing a *panoramic view* of God's revelation, the Bible, concerning His *vision, plan, purpose, and strategy* for advancement and actualization of the divine mission clearly presented in the scriptures. This mission hinges on God's *Thesis Statement* in Genesis 3:15, which I will give lengthy analysis. Here God sums up His *vision, plan, and purpose* for restoring man to a right relationship with Himself. I will also critically examine His *strategy of execution* and how *every believer* is a *key player* in God's *strategy* for realization of His *vision, plan, and purpose*. God's *strategy of execution* is capsuled and condensed in Matthew 28:16-20, the Great Commission! As we, together, study the very words of God, we will expose key hermeneutical principles that will guide us in ferreting out, or exegeting, the truth. The hermeneutical principle we will highlight, while employing others, is called *The Law of First Mention*.

Neither space nor time would permit me to list those to whom I owe a mountainous debt for their contributions to my life, and therefore, to this book.

I am in heavy debt to a plethora of authors who have written according to the light the Spirit of God has cast upon their hearts in the illumination of His word.

I am in debt to a daunting list of preachers, bible teachers, and authors who have exposed me to volumes of truth during my Christian life. This includes men like, Martin Luther, Philipp Melanchthon, Augustine of Hippo, Nicholas Ridley, John Owen, Richard Baxter, Bishop J.C. Ryle, Arthur Pink, Augustus Toplady, John Bunyan, CS Lewis, John Stott, John Whitcomb, Dana and Mante, Gerhard Kittle, Martyn Lloyd Jones, C.H. Spurgeon, Bob Morey, Arnold Fruchtenbaum, Voddie Baucham, Ray Vander Laan, and last, but far from least, John MacArthur. I am in debt to the men who the Lord has given me the privilege to train and equip as "disciples" over the past 30+ years. Their numbers have multiplied far beyond my wildest expectations.

I am indebted to my high school History Teacher, the late Clay Markum. His knowledge and manner of teaching History, with his conversation-styled illustrations, captured me as a high school sophomore. The resulting love he stimulated in me for, both, historical information and his style of illustrating truth continues to flow through my very being.

I would be remiss if I didn't express the debt I owe my Dad, William Emmanuel Douglas. He had a voracious thirst for the printed word, and could not get enough of it. He once told me "Whatever you do, never underestimate the value of reading. Read widely, including opposing views, so that you know what to believe." As a young boy, my family lived in a house heated by a wood stove. I vividly remember my Dad making a fire first thing every morning. On one occasion, at 5am, I remember my Dad standing before the open door of the wood stove reading the newspaper that he was about to burn to start the fire. I remember my Mom saying, "Manuel, are you going to start the fire, or just stand there reading the paper instead?" As I sit here writing in my home office, it occurs to me that the reason I'm surrounded by 3 large bookshelves filled with theological books, doctrinal books, multiple biographies of Reformation leaders, engineering literature, music, etc. is because of the model and advice my Dad provided me. He has been with the Lord since 1982, but I continue to live that model.

I am in particularly crushing debt to my "Paul", Brother Herb Hodges, who is now in the presence of the Lord watching his eternal dividends continue to multiply through me and the countless thousands of men God used him to train and equip. He, in an up-close and personal way, transferred his life into mine through

8

literally thousands of hours of teaching, fellowship, love, and on-the-job training, while traveling the globe discipling pastors and church leaders.

I owe my very ministry presence to my discipler and best friend of 30+ years, Roy "Soup" Campbell. As my Pastor in my early walk, he strapped me to himself and refused to give up on me. At times he must have thought, "Who will deliver me from this body of death?" When the deacons of the church he pastored, collectively, demanded that he boot me out of the church he declared, "You are going to leave him alone, and I'm going to teach him the word. Know this, if he goes, I go!"

I owe a debt of gratitude to Dr. Kurt Kilpatrick, professor of Old Testament and Hebrew, Mid America Seminary, for reviewing some of this work.

I owe a debt of great gratitude to my Pastor, John Nickolas, for spending time helping me with priceless reviews.

I am in heavy debt to my dear Disciple-Making Brother, Dr. Dan Baugh, for providing review and invaluable feedback.

I owe a tremendous debt of gratitude to my friend and disciple, John Langel Sr., without whom this work may have never even started. After sitting in on my teaching sessions, John asked if I had ever thought about writing a book, and I told him that I didn't think that I was qualified to do so. He laughed at me. When he stopped laughing, he disclosed the truth that he had worked for years helping with such endeavors and would help me as I discipled him.

I owe a great debt of appreciation to Charlie Liebert for his incredible guidance in helping me edit and publish this book.

I owe an unpayable debt of gratitude to my wife, Amy, who endured countless hours being bereft of my attention and presence as she loved, served, and supported me while I studied, wrote, rewrote, and edited.

To all of these and others, I extend my deepest appreciation and gratitude; I defer their reward to the Judgment Seat of Christ, who will bestow riches upon them beyond all I could ask or think.

Finally, I thank the Lord Jesus Christ for loving me and allowing one such as I to, in a feeble way, contribute to the equipping of His Saints for the work of ministry for His glory.

I pray you will see, understand, and implement, Jesus' *vision, plan, purpose, strategy, and command to action* applied in your life. His command to action is to YOU, directly and personally. Do you dare risk standing before Him at the Bema Seat (2 Corinthians 5:10) to receive reward for your Christian service having ignored or disregarded the only command to action that He gave you? As you begin to read this book you may be able to truthfully say that you're not aware of your personal role in advancing the program, plan, and purpose of our Potentate, nor how to perform it. However, when you've finished this book, that will no longer be the case.

Jim Douglas

Table of Contents

Preface

Anyone who has been in Christian leadership for any appreciable length of time knows that most Christians have a bad sense of Spiritual *self-worth*. The primary reason for this is that they make no meaningful contribution to the cause of Christ that fulfills, satisfies, and gratifies them. Tradition says that activities such as ushering, collecting the offering, baking the communion bread, removing snow from the parking lot, singing in the choir, hanging decorations for the Christmas cantata, making costumes for the Easter production, attending the mission meals, and things like these, belong in the category of *ministry*. These activities are part of oiling and maintaining the machinery of the institutional church.

> **The biblical strategy for gospel advance has been subtlety, but radically, altered from "Go and tell" to "Come and hear".**

The biblical strategy for gospel advance has been subtlety, but radically, altered from "Go and tell" to "Come and hear". For example, every biblical symbol for gospel advance contains the idea of *penetration* and going *out*. The mighty mandate of our Lord Jesus to each of His followers, *The Great Commission*, assumes this. The word *"go"*, in Matthew 28:19, is a present circumstantial participle in English. It is better translated *as you are going, or since you are going, or while you are going.* The directional idea of gospel advance is always *out!* Consider gospel symbols in the scriptures. For example, in Matthew 5:13 Jesus describes Christians as *the salt of the earth.* Salt is of no use as long as it remains *in* the shaker! Let me recommend a great book based on this very concept and this very passage (Matthew 5:13). It is a book on Evangelism, written by Becky Pippert, entitled *Out of the Saltshaker.* The salt must get out of the shaker and *penetrate,* or it is of no value. Salt is a preservative, promotes healing, and is an irritant when it comes in

12

contact with an open wound. These are attributes of Christians under the figure of *salt.*

> **Notice, Jesus did *not* say *"you are the light of the church.* No! He said, "you are the light of the world."**

Let's consider gospel advance under the symbol of *light.* Stick with the book of Matthew chapter 5, verse 14-16. Here Jesus described Christians as follows, "You are the light of the world. A city set on a hill cannot be hidden; nor does anyone light a lamp and put it under a basket, but on the lampstand, and it gives light to all who are in the house. Let your light shine before men in such a way that they may see your good works, and glorify your Father who is in heaven." Notice, Jesus did *not* say *"you are the light of the church."* No! He said, "you are the light of the world." Again, this symbol is one of *penetration.* Light pierces the darkness and drives it away. You have never seen darkness refuse to yield to the light! However, per Jesus in this text, if the light is placed in, or under, something, it is totally ineffective for the purpose it exists. Given this massive truth, it egregious when Pastors and church leaders spend the majority of their time encouraging Christians to "invite your friends and family *to* church." What a tragedy! This is commensurate to saying that, if there's no building to invite people *to,* you can't know Christ! This is just the opposite of God's strategy for gospel advance. Instead of training and equipping the Saints to do the work of the ministry *as they are going,* we expect the lost man to come to us! This is the subtle, soul-damning change from *go and tell to come and hear.* If your church leadership, structure and worship are in lock-step with the scripture, there is absolutely *nothing* that would cause the lost man to want to come there!!! That's why it is prevalent to have leadership, structure, and worship that are *not* in lock-step with the proscriptions of the Bible in order to attract the lost man. So, we

13

employ rock musicians, smoke machines, dim lights, vestibule coffee houses, interpretive dance, and 15-minute *sermonettes* to try and draw lost people to the building!

I really cannot leave this thought without reference to Matthew 9:36-38. Here we read, "Seeing the people, He (Jesus) felt compassion for them, because they were distressed like sheep without a shepherd. Then He said to His disciples, the harvest is plentiful, but the workers are few. Therefore, beseech the Lord of the harvest to send out workers into His harvest." Notice that Jesus said, "pray to the Lord of the harvest to *send out workers into His harvest.*" Now, skip down to Matthew 10:5 and read, "These twelve Jesus *sent out after instructing them*;" (emphasis mine). The Christians that Jesus commanded to pray that God would send workers *out* into His harvest (Matthew 9:36-38), became the workers that He sent *out* into His harvest (Matthew 10:5)! I grew up on a farm in Kentucky. I have never seen a farmer stand in the door of the barn and invite the harvest to join him inside; but that is exactly what is happening in today's institutional church, instead of equipping and *sending out workers into His harvest!* We do not say this, but by our actions, we convey a distinct message. What is the message? *Come to the building, hear the gospel, have an opportunity to go to heaven, OR stay away and go to hell!* We have changed the method of gospel advance from *go and tell to come and hear!* Because we refuse to follow the Savior's strategy, we must employ the aforementioned activities to draw a crowd and have them feel "welcome". Since these activities fly in the face of the Savior's Strategy, the *lost* crowd feels welcome, but God certainly does not! There is no thought of whether *God feels welcome in the place that is supposed to represent Him!* Hebrews 12:29 says, "Our God is a consuming fire..." I'll add that *we* are the fuel for the flames!

A couple of these activities are actually necessary, but fall woefully short of being classified as what the Bible describes as *ministry*. When Walmart has snow removed from their parking lot they call it a contract, while the church calls the same necessary function *ministry*. Most of these *activities* advance the reputation of the organization or the individual, but do little, if anything, to advance the total global cause of Christ. Believers subconsciously know this, which leads to a bad sense of Spiritual self-worth. The scant few Christians involved in these *activities* are constantly assured by the leadership that they are rendering invaluable service to the Lord. However, I submit that these believers are *dedicated* to *duty* that misses the mark of *devotion and obedience* to the Master. Yet we pray over these *activities* that God will bless them and use them for His glory, as if these things somehow come under the heading of obedience to the King of Kings! One can only muse about the look on God's face when He hears prayers like, "Lord, we give you the bus ministry, and the greeter ministry, and the choir ministry, and the car repair ministry, and the usher ministry. Please use these for your glory and to build your kingdom." Search the scripture; you will not find any such artificial activities included in the petitions of the Apostle Paul, nor those of the Apostle Peter, nor any other writer of scripture, nor those used mightily by the Lord to advance His kingdom! What, in the name of heaven, are we doing?

Before the God Who sees you, ask yourself three piercing questions:

1. If God were to answer every one of your personal prayers, what would be the impact on the total global cause of Jesus Christ?

2. All Christians must appear before the Lord at the Judgment Seat of Christ. 2 Corinthians 5:10 says, "For we (all Christians) must all appear before the judgment seat of Christ, so that each one may be recompensed for his deeds in the body, according to what he has done, whether good or bad." When believers see the word *bad* in this verse, they tend to take it out of context and equate this with

sin. They typically imagine that the Lord is going to display their individual sin on a giant screen, and everyone will know their private failures. Nothing could be further from the truth! First, the believer's sins were paid for at the cross of Calvary by the Lord Himself. So, this is not a judgment on sin. The Greek word for *judgment* is *Bema*. This is a word for *reward*. The Greek word translated *bad* is the word *phaulus*. It is a word that describes *value.*

The Lord is going to evaluate everything you've done since becoming a Christian. The evaluation will be to determine whether what you did (your Christian service) was of value to the Lord, or merely worthless to the Lord. If that service was *good* (from God's perspective) then you will receive a reward. If that which *you* called *ministry* is deemed *worthless* by the Lord, it will be burned up. 1 Corinthians 3:10-15 says, "According to the grace of God which was given to me, like a wise master builder I laid a foundation, and another is building on it. But each man must be careful how he builds on it. For no man can lay a foundation other than the one which is laid, which is Jesus Christ. Now If any man builds on the foundation with gold, silver, precious stones, wood, hay, straw, each man's work will become evident; for the day will show it because it is to be revealed with fire, and the fire itself will test the quality of each man's work. If any man's work which he has built on it remains, he will receive a reward. If any man's work is burned up, he will suffer loss; but he himself will be saved, yet so as through fire."

Therefore, the *works* that you did as a Christian will be evaluated by the Lord, and that deemed worthless will burn up at the Judgment Seat of Christ. Eternity will tell how large your pile of ashes will be, though you will be saved. You see, the Lord is not at all interested in how large your pile of ashes may be. He's *not* in eternity just waiting to ignite the flames with what *you* consider to

16

be *ministry*. Jesus would greatly prefer that you obey His command and *there* be able to heap tremendous eternal rewards upon you! However, because we've accepted Satan's Subtle Substitute, and built with wood, hay, and stubble, as opposed to gold, silver and precious stone, the ash pile will be significant for most believers. Given that truth, at the Judgment Seat of Christ, what will be your answer if Jesus simply places His Great Commission before your eyes, and asks "What did you do in obedience to this command?"

> **Are we following the Savior's strategy or Satan's subtle substitute?**

3. Since Jesus commanded each of His followers to Make Disciples of all nations (literally *ethnic groups*) how, specifically, do any of the activities listed above advance His mandate? Given the fact that one-half of the human race has never heard the name of Christ, we must jettison tradition, and critically reexamine our manual of operation (the Bible) if we're to obey the *mandate*, pursue the *mission*, and employ the *methodology* of the *Master*! The *mandate* is the Great Commission, which contains the command to *make disciples*. The *mission* is world evangelization that addresses every ethnic group. The *methodology* is intentional, personal, hands-on training and equipping less mature believers to reproduce disciples - not converts.

The purpose for writing this book is to cause the people of God to shine the light of in-context scripture on the *activities* that we hold as *sacred,* and compare those things to the mandate that Jesus gave to each of the subjects of His Kingdom. Most germane to this purpose is to exhort, encourage, and/or provoke the people of God to become students of His very word. When we honestly do this, we will discover whether we are following the *Savior's Strategy,* or *Satan's Subtle Substitute.*

Introduction

God's mandate, mission, and methodology for world evangelization (missions) through reproductive Disciple Making, as recorded throughout the Bible, is the focus of this work. The Bible records the most succinct, comprehensive statement of this plan, and strategy. In Matthew 28:16-20 from the lips of our Lord Jesus Christ. This text contains one verb of command given to each of Jesus' followers. That command is to *make disciples* of all ethnic groups. All obedience to this command must have total *world vision;* the contemporary church's focus on its local *community* is deliberate disobedience and a vote against the strategy of Jesus!

> **You see, *converts* grow *old* in the Lord. *Disciples* grow *up* in the Lord and reproduce.**

Most believers would interpret this command, *make disciples,* to mean *make converts*; if that's what our Lord meant He would've said that. You see, *converts* grow *old* in the Lord. *Disciples* grow *up* in the Lord and reproduce. Still others would interpret the word *disciple* to be synonymous with the word *Christian.* That is not what our Lord commanded. The word *Christian* is a wonderful word. It is a Hebrew idea (Messiah), a Greek word (Christus), with a Latin ending (ianus). The Latin ending means a *slave in the household of.* For example, a *Caesarianus* would be a slave in the household of Caesar. Likewise, a *Christianus* would be a slave in the household of Christ. Wouldn't it be awesome if followers of Christ actually exhibited the lifestyle suggested by this word!

As wonderful as this word *Christian* is it is only used three times in the Bible (Acts 11:26; Acts 26:28; 1 Peter 4:16) In each of these passages we find the spirit of derision, as the term is employed by enemies of the faith and never by a friend. This word, *Christian,* is one that believers continuously use in nearly every setting of daily life. In contrast, the word *disciple* appears 269 times in the first five books of the New Testament! Now, don't hurry past that fact; let that soak in. How many times does the author of scripture, the Holy Spirit, have to say something for it to be etched in eternity in the mind of God? Once! So, when HE repeats Himself 268 times it must be that God wants us to catch up with and major on the term, the definition, and the concept! Do you get the picture? The word *Christian*, coined by enemies, is used perpetually, and only appears 3 times in the Bible; the word *disciple,* hammered by the Holy Spirit, appears 269 times in the first 5 books of the New Testament, and rarely used, in its context, by believers! We've been duped! As previously stated, the word *Christian* is a good word. However, the greatest enemy of the *best* is *never* the *worst*, but the *good*!

The reason we know that Christ's command to *make disciples* could not mean *make Christians* is that the term (Christian) doesn't appear in the New Testament until *after* our Lord has ascended! It seems the contemporary church is confused as to the very definition of the word *disciple;* since this is the case, there's little wonder why we're woefully deficient in obeying our Lord's command to reproduce disciples!

Perhaps you've seen the wall placard that says, *"The main thang is to keep the main thang the main thang!"* The contemporary church has radically deviated from this profound ethic. Upon careful, Biblical examination, this is evident in so many areas of practice. We've even replaced the terminology of Jesus' command to *make disciples* with the term *discipleship.* With this subtle replacement of terms comes a not-so-subtle change in the definition of the word *disciple,* and a change in *methodology* for obeying the command.

> **Disciple making is done by *persons*, and not by *programs***

19

A few years ago, I visited a church in my home state of Kentucky. I was handed a church bulletin, which I perused prior to the start of corporate worship. One of the announcements in this bulletin read as follows: "Discipleship - Wednesday evenings 6-7:30 for six weeks." Since the model of Disciple Making left by the Lord of glory, creator of the universe, involves intense, close-up, training and *life transference,* with twelve men for approximately three years, it is blasphemously presumptuous to even suggest this six-week, hour and a half meeting to be obedience to His command. This is not *discipling,* but mere *dabbling!* Disciple making is done by *persons,* and not by *programs.* It is done by *men and women*, and not by *materials.* Compare this 9-hour, sterile, class to the countless hours and expense related to the perpetual, feverish, frustrating, eternally irrelevant, activity of the typical church.

My Discipler, Herb Hodges said it better than I can, so I'll quote him at this point. He said, "It is evident to me that we Christians must re-study the New Testament, our manual of operation, and we must force ourselves to be ruthlessly objective as we do. We must declare ourselves independent of tradition and find out what the New Testament tells us about ourselves and our God-given assignment." This quote is found in the introduction of Herb's excellent book on disciple making, Tally Ho the Fox, which I highly recommend.

I'm reminded of a story at this point. Many years ago, a Bible Teacher was teaching on the Great Commission. At the end of the lecture, he engaged the auditors to play a game. He said, "I have something in my pocket that nobody has ever seen before. I'm going to take it out, and let all of you see it, then it will disappear and nobody will ever see it again. Can you guess what it is?" The audience started randomly firing out guesses; the longer it went the wilder the guesses became! Finally, the teacher stopped the guessing exercise. He reached into his shirt pocket and pulled out a peanut still in the shell. He said, "Inside this shell is something nobody has ever seen before." He cracked open the shell and held the peanut up for all to see. Then, he said, "In a moment, nobody will ever see it again." He then popped it in his mouth and ate it; and nobody ever saw it again!

More than 2000 years ago, the Lord pulled out of His heart the command to make disciples of all nations. His strategy worked wonderfully for the first two centuries. Then, Satan raised up subtle substitutes to offset the Savior's strategy. Now, it is as if the Savior's strategy has disappeared - never to be the *norm* again for the body of Christ!

We must return to the mandate, mission, and methodology of the Master, which is guaranteed to produce eternal dividends. C.S. Lewis said it like this, "All that is not eternal is eternally out of date." In Matthew 28:20 Jesus promised to attend us with His personal presence as we follow His plan when He said, "Lo, I am with you always, even to the end of the age." This promise is not to be taken out of context to mean that the Lord will never leave nor forsake the Christian. Hebrews 13:5, and other passages promise that to all believers. No, this promise, in context, is exclusively for His followers that are engaged in pursuing His mandate, fulfilling His mission, using His methodology, according to His strategy in obedience to Him as Master! This book invites, and implores, you to join in an independent of tradition, ruthlessly objective, in-context, re-study of the very words of God to determine the *main thang* in obedience to our Lord's command to *make disciples of all nations.*

Chapter 1 In Pursuit of Truth

It is the universal cry of man's soul to worship, and *everyone* worships something or someone. If they don't worship the One, true God – the God of the Bible, they worship false gods, favorite gurus, things, or even themselves. Another universal longing in man's soul is the search for *Truth*. Man, inherently, looks for the source of truth, justice, morality, meaning, and beauty. If we adopt the Eastern, way of pursuing truth and look within ourselves to find out what is true and what God is like, we immediately fall into the quagmire of relativism. Whatever god, gods or goddesses we find, do not exist independent of how we conceive them. Whatever *Truth* we find introspectively is subjective, and thus cannot be a *universal* in defining *Truth*. Once again, we sink into the quagmire of relativism. This is just as futile as Western Greek philosophers, such as Socrates, Plato, Aristotle, Sigmund Freud, the Roman Seneca, and others, who looked within themselves for the knowledge of God and *truth*. They finally concluded that *man* is the measure of all things, including *God, truth, justice, morality, meaning, and beauty*.

If we decide that we must look outside of ourselves for the knowledge of God and *truth*, then we will either look *down, across, or up*.

Looking Down

We look *down* when we try to find God and *truth* in something that is intrinsically less than what we are. To look to insects, animals, birds, trees, the environment, or *mother earth*, as the *origin* of truth is absurd because they are not *cognitive egos* who can say, *I Am*. Thus, they are intrinsically inferior to man who, as a cognitive ego can say, *I Am*. *Pantheism* is actually a form of *Atheism* in that it denies the existence of the God of the Bible who created the world out of nothing (Greek - ex nihilo) and exists apart from and independent of His creation. After denying the existence of God, pantheism takes the word *God* and applies it to the world. But the god of pantheism is not a personal God who hears and answers prayer. The god of pantheism, this universal *force,* is intrinsically less than what we are because it is not a cognitive ego. Such a god is incapable of knowledge, will, or emotion. Accordingly, pantheism's *it* cannot be a sufficient basis for the knowledge of God, truth, justice, morality, meaning, and beauty, because an *I Am is always superior to an it*!

To see man's overwhelming per chant for *Pantheism,* all one need do is look at the 2009 James Cameron movie, *Avatar.* This Sci-Fi adventure, which I found most entertaining, represents the height of *Pantheism* with a good helping of *Animism* thrown in for good measure. In this setting a former Marine, paralyzed from the waist down by war, and a crew of scientists, travel from a decaying, resource-depleted Earth to the distant, forest-covered moon, Pandora, in the year 2154. Just to give you a flavor of why I cite *Avatar* as a modern-day example of Pantheism, I'll quote from one of the world's leading movie critics, *Rolling Stone Magazine.* "Just as the storyline involving the decimation of an indigenous population parallels early American history, so too the Na'vi's spiritual beliefs often parallel those of Native American religions. The Na'vi worship a goddess known as Eywa, the Great Mother, a deity that seems both personal (the Na'vi pray to her) as well as encompassing the collective energy of Pandora's living things. Thus, the Na'vi exhibit high reverence for all plants and animals." And, as mentioned, the film's environmental message is set against this spiritual backdrop. The trees, the forests and everything in them are not merely part of a natural ecology, but a spiritual one. Accordingly, the violence perpetrated against Pandora's creatures is not merely a physical violation, but a spiritual affront too.

The Na'vi's holiest place is the Tree of Souls. Its airborne seeds are referred to as "pure spirits." Its branches—more luminous tendrils

23

than bark-covered limbs—are used in prayer rituals. Twice the Na'vi gather before this tree in what could be described as services of corporate healing and worship. In the first, they petition Eywa to save the wounded earthling, Dr. Augustine, by transferring her soul from her human body into her avatar. The tribe's spiritual leader, a female shaman (and the character, Neytiri's, mother), says, "The Great Mother may choose to save all that she is in this body." She then prays, "Hear us please, All Mother. ... Let her walk among us as one of the people." Amid those prayers, Augustine tells Jake, "I'm with her [Eywa]. She's real." A similar service later involves *Jake's* attempt to become fully Na'vi. Both times, the tribe is seated, undulating and chanting ecstatically.

The Na'vi at times listen to the whispering voices of deceased ancestors. And they psychically bond with flying, almost dragon-like creatures, known as banshees. During a funeral service, Neytiri tells Jake, "All energy is only borrowed. ... You have to give it back." Neytiri says of the Na'vi's initiation ceremony, *"Every person is born twice. The second time is when you earn your place among the people forever."* Jake eventually prays to Eywa, telling her that the humans are about to destroy the Tree of Souls. Neytiri responds, "Our Great Mother does not take sides, Jake. She protects only the balance of life." [*Spoiler Warning*] But when the planet's creatures come to the Na'vi's rescue in the final battle, Neytiri exults that Eywa has answered Jake's prayers."

This epitome of *Pantheism* remains one of the highest earning movies in history, raking in $2.8B (for a $300M investment) at the Box Office. To see how such outrageous, anti-God, fantasy has affected our culture, all one need do is look at the fanaticism of the current *Climate Change* movement that is more than willing to sacrifice people in favor of saving *Mother Earth!* Michael J. Fox once said, "The ant at my picnic has the same right to life as my child." Incidentally, this same actor is one of the leading advocates for using aborted fetuses for stem-cell research in hopes of curing his Parkinson's Disease condition! Here you have an obvious Pantheist conflicting his worldview. "The ant has a right to life, but that baby doesn't if its remnants could lead to curing my physical condition!" Billionaires are advocating reducing the population of people in order to save the planet; The next step (a short one) will be deciding which members of the population are expendable! This is a direct affront to the God of the universe, as it ascribes deity and worship, not to Him, but to His creation. Animal Rights Activists flood the airways with appeals for donations to save animals, while they are content to walk past God's *image bearers* sleeping on the park bench and going hungry. Romans 1:21-25 says, "For even though they knew God, they did not honor Him as God or give thanks, but they became futile in their speculations, and their foolish heart was darkened. Professing to be wise, they became fools, and exchanged the glory of the incorruptible God for an image in the form of corruptible man and of birds and four-footed animals and crawling creatures. Therefore, God gave them over in the lusts of their hearts to impurity, so that their bodies would be dishonored among them. For they exchanged the truth of God for a lie, and worshiped and served the creature rather than the Creator, who is blessed forever. Amen." If you want to see more results of this defiance of God, read Romans 1:26-2:8. Further, *Pantheism* diminishes the importance of God's highest creation signature, made in His very image – man! This is a sterling example of man *looking down* in search of God, truth, justice, morality, meaning, and beauty.

Looking Across

We look *across* when we assume that some fellow human being is the one who can tell us all about God and *truth*. It does not matter if he is an Eastern guru, a cult leader, or a psychic. Each of these is a finite human being that has been exalted, and thus, cannot become the infinite origin of information about God and *truth*. He/she is only a finite creature and makes mistakes and errors just like the rest of us. Romans 3:23 tells us, "*All* have sinned and fall short of the glory of God." This means that If you are less perfect than God you are a flawed sinner; welcome to the human race - you qualify!

The list of these false teachers and cult leaders is too large to exhaust. This list includes people like,

Scientology founder, Elrond Hubbard; The Church of Christ, Scientist founder; Mary Baker Eddy: Mormonism founder, Joseph Smith, and his successor, Brigham Young; Seventh Day Adventist founder, Ellen G. White; Branch Davidian founder, David Koresh; Unification Church founder, Sun Myung Moon. (This Cult Leader was defended by no less than Jerry Falwell – Head of Moral Majority and Joseph Lowery – head of the Southern Christian Leadership Conference, Harvey Cox – Professor of Divinity at Harvard, and Democratic Senator Eugene McCarthy.) We simply must include Peoples Temple and Jonestown Guyana founder, Jim Jones.

This list of false teachers and false Messiahs, would be incomplete without the inclusion of the denomination-acclaimed "Vicar of Christ", the Pope, head of the Catholic Church, and sovereign of the Vatican City State. The Bible never even suggests that any human being is to be considered "Christ on earth",

The respective, personal opinions, and esoteric interpretations of *truth* by all of these people are just as subjective and flawed as ours. Romans 3:22b-23 says, "Without distinction, ALL have sinned and fall short of the glory of God" (emphasis mine). Thus, they are only *equal* to us, and hence, cannot provide a sufficient basis for an accurate knowledge of God and *truth*. This is a sterling example of man *looking across* in search of God, truth, justice, morality, meaning, and beauty.

Looking Up

Finally, we look *up* when we identify the origin as a deity or deities who are above us. The ancient Babylonians, Assyrians, Egyptians, Greeks, and Romans worshipped a multitude of finite deities who were only *man writ large.* These finite deities were human in every respect, because they were inventions of man's imagination. They lied, cheated, and stole because they reflected the corrupt human society in which they were concocted and worshipped. Since they fought and quarreled among themselves, the gods could not provide mankind with an infinite, immutable standard for truth, justice, morality, meaning or beauty. As finite creatures, they themselves were also in search of a universal authority to explain these things and themselves.

The *upward look,* to the God of the Bible, is the sole, foolproof source where truth can be found. The only way to know God personally, and to know about God intellectually, is through His self-revelation as given in Holy Scripture. The attempt to define God and truth on any other basis than a careful exegesis of scripture is the mother of all heresy and cultism. Only the Bible speaks of an infinite, personal, triune God who is the origin of truth, justice, morality, meaning, and beauty. This triune God speaks to us in the Bible by the singular "I" and the plural "We" at the same time without falling into the errors of Unitarianism or polytheism. He is the source of *truth!*

Despite **contemporary thought,** *Truth* **is not** *relative. Truth* is objective, and it is absolute. *Truth is what the infinite, omniscient, omnipotent, omnipresent, God of the Bible says it is!* It is not what I think, nor what you think. It is not what we collectively think. It is not what we hope, wish, surmise, feel, or deduce; **Truth is** *only* **what God says!** In John 14:6 Jesus said, "I am the way, the truth, and the life. No man comes to the Father, but by Me." Romans 3:4

says, "May it never be! Let God be found true, though every man be found a liar, as it is written, That You may be justified in Your words, and prevail when You are judged." So, absolute truth is based on the very words of God as found in the Bible.

The Apostle Peter was a stalwart proponent of the historicity, authority, authenticity, and veracity of the Bible. In his second letter in chapter 1:16-20 he gave us a brief apologetic on why we can trust the Bible. There we read, "For we did not follow cleverly devised tales when we made known to you the power and coming of our Lord Jesus Christ, but we were eyewitnesses of His majesty. For when He received honor and glory from God the Father, such an utterance as this was made to Him by the Majestic Glory, 'This is My Beloved Son with whom I am well-pleased' and we ourselves heard this utterance made from heaven when we were with Him on the holy mountain. So, we have the prophetic word made more sure, to which you do well to pay attention as to a lamp shining in a dark place, until the day dawns and the morning star arises in your hearts. But know this first of all, that no prophecy of Scripture is a matter of one's own interpretation, for no prophecy was ever made by an act of human will, but men moved by the Holy Spirit spoke from God."

To paraphrase Peter, "We were there; We saw Him pull back that human epidermis and His glory shown through. We heard the voice of the Father, from heaven, proclaiming Jesus to be His very Son! This supernatural experience was breath-taking! But, Peter says, as awesome as that was, we have something greater than that. We have the very words of God. These very words of God are more sure than *any* experience, and you'd do well to pay crucial, critical heed to it just as you would a light shining in a dark place! Psalm 119:105 says, "Thy word is a lamp unto my feet and a light unto my path." This is a sterling example of man *looking up,* to the God of the universe, in search of God, truth, justice, morality, meaning, and beauty.

Peter is defending belief in the Bible! Let's dissect Peter's statement a bit. I'll begin by giving you an astute summation of why we can believe and trust the Bible. Many giant theologians of the past, such as, Martin Luther, John Calvin, C.H. Spurgeon, Puritan Richard Baxter, have preached and made summary statements about why we can believe the Bible. Many awesome contemporary theologians, such as, Dr. R.C. Sproul, Dr. John MacArthur, Dr. D. Martyn Lloyd-Jones, J.I. Packer, and Andrew Murray, have all preached, and made definitive, summary statements about why we can believe the Bible – why the Bible is inerrant.

In my humble opinion, the Chancellor of African Christian University in Lusaka, Zambia, Dr. Voddie Baucham, gave the most succinct summary statement, that I've heard or read, of why we can believe the Bible. He said, *"The Bible is a reliable collection of historical documents written down by eye witnesses during the lifetime of other eye witnesses. They report to us supernatural events that took place in fulfillment of specific prophecies and claim to be divine rather than human in origin."* We will apply this laser-focused summation of why we can believe the Bible to Peter's statement about the word of God, in 2 Peter 1:16-20.

Chapter 2 Validating Eternal Truth

There are four components required to validate truth; they are Historicity, Authority, Authenticity, and Veracity. Through application of this universally recognized multi-criteria decision analysis (MCDA) we shall establish why we can believe the Bible to be true.

The Historicity of the Bible

The first of the four required components for validation of eternal truth is *Historicity*. Let us start here with the definition. *Historicity* is the historical actuality of persons and events, meaning the quality of being part of history as opposed to being a historical myth, legend, or fiction. *Historicity* denotes historical actuality, authenticity, factuality and focuses on the *true* value of knowledge claims about the past. Relative to the events of the text Peter asserts, first of all, that the Bible is a reliable collection of historical documents. Peter says, "For we did not follow cleverly devised tales when we made known to you the power and coming of our Lord Jesus Christ." In other words, when we told you about Jesus, we did not share with you, myths or fairy tales or legends. To paraphrase, Peter is saying, we were sharing factual information with you. These things actually happened. Next Peter says, "But we were eyewitnesses of his majesty." Man, we saw it. We were there on the holy mountain and witnessed this!

Incidentally, the Apostle John was part of the *we* on that occasion. He corroborates Peter's account in 1 John 1:1,2 where he writes, "That which was from the beginning, what we have heard, what we have seen with our eyes, what we have looked at and touched with our hands, concerning the Word of Life. And the life was manifested, and we have seen and testify and proclaim to you the eternal life, which was with the Father and was manifested to us. What we have seen and heard we proclaim to you also."

In Matthew 18:16 Jesus said, "…But if he will not hear you, then take with you one or two more, that in the mouth of two or three witnesses every word may be established." Here, Jesus drew from Deuteronomy 19:15, which says, "A single witness shall not rise up against a man on account of any iniquity or any sin which he has committed; on the evidence of two or three witnesses a matter shall be confirmed."

The Mount of Transfiguration event is described by Matthew in 17:1-9 this way. "And after six days Jesus took Peter, James, and John his brother, and brought them up into a high mountain. And was transfigured before them: and His face did shine as the sun, and His raiment was white as the light. And, behold, there appeared unto them Moses and Elijah talking with Him. Then Peter said unto Jesus, Lord, it is good for us to be here: if it is your will, let us make here three tabernacles; one for you, and one for Moses, and one for Elijah. While Peter was yet speaking, behold a bright cloud overshadowed them: and behold a voice out of the cloud which said, this is my beloved Son, in Whom I am well pleased; Listen to Him. And when the disciples heard it, they fell on their faces, and were afraid. And Jesus came and touched them and said Arise, and be not afraid. And when they had lifted up their eyes, they saw no man, except Jesus only. And as they came down from the mountain, Jesus charged them saying, 'Tell the vision to no one, until the Son of Man rises again from the dead.'" So, the combination of the respective testimonies of Peter, John, and Matthew, about the Mount of Transfiguration event, meet the Biblical criterion for eye witness corroboration! (1)

Man, there is something about eye witness accounts. When my daughter, Jayme, was about 3 years old I taught her that she should never open the refrigerator without permission. One day as I was sitting in the family room, I heard the refrigerator door open, and knew it had to be Jayme, as she and I were the only ones in the house. I got up and peeked around the kitchen door and, sure enough, there she was standing in front of the open refrigerator door. I quietly went back to my seat in the family room, and called her to come to me

. I asked her if she had been in the refrigerator, to which she replied, "No Daddy. I not in the fidgerator." I said, "Honey, Daddy can punish you for lying, or for going into the refrigerator. So, I'll ask again. Before you answer, you need to know that I saw you there." She looked up with tears welling up in her eyes and said, "Daddy, I love you". Now, she was totally unaware of the glob of jelly spilled on her shirt just below her chin that would've betrayed her anyway! Still, the point is that there is something highly compelling about eyewitness accounts. John said, "We have seen it with our eyes." And when we consider the gospels and the epistles they were written during the age of disproof. The *Historicity* of the Bible is supported by eye witnesses.

Next, the *Historicity* of the Bible is confirmed by the narrative itself identifying other historically validated occurrences that happened at the same time of the biblical event. For example, Luke places the birth of Jesus Christ at the exact time of historically validated events. In Luke 2:1-7 we read, "Now in those days a decree went out from Caesar August that a census be taken of all the inhabited earth. This was the first census taken while Quirinius was governor of Syria. And everyone was on his way to register for the census, each to his own city. Joseph also went up from Galilee, from the city of Nazareth, to Judea, the city of David which is called Bethlehem, because he was of the house and family of David, in order to register along with Mary, who was engaged to him, and was with child. While they were there the days were completed for her to give birth. And she gave birth to her first-born son; and she wrapped Him in cloths and laid Him in a manger, because there was no room for them in the inn."

> **This is why *context* is critical in discerning what God says in His word.**

A historical background is in order here. Caesar Augustus was given the name 'Caius Octavius' when he was formally adopted by Julius Caesar. He was Julius Caesar's grand-nephew, adopted son, and primary heir to Julius Caesar's throne. By the way, *adoption* in most cultures, including ours, does not carry the same connotations as it did in the Roman culture. In Roman culture, *adoption* was an honored status. A biologically born son could be dispossessed, or even killed, by the father without recourse or penalty; Not so with an *adopted* son! His status and inheritance were permanent. This is why *context* is critical in discerning what God says in His word. Did you ever wonder why the Bible teaches that we are not only *born from above*, but also *adopted*? The *new birth* gives us the *divine nature* of Christ (2 Peter 1:4). Adoptive parents can give the child love, resources, and an inheritance, but not their own distinct characteristics; Their characteristics are passed on through biological birth. *Adoption* gives us full adult standing, full adult responsibility, and full, irrevocable, inheritance! Nine of the thirteen Caesars were adopted! So, Octavius was *adopted* as a son by Julius Caesar for the express purpose of becoming his successor! (2)

Before and after Julius' death, in 44 B.C., the Roman government was constantly torn by power struggles. This is evident by the historical account of how Julius Caesar died at the hands of a group of Roman Senators on 15 March 44 B.C. This murderous group, led by Cassius, included Mark Antony and Julius' good friend, Brutus. Julius was caught totally by surprise in this ambush. As they drove their knives of treachery and betrayal into his body, Julius was shocked to find his friend and confidante, Brutus, among the conspirators. This was captured by Shakespeare in the famous question on Julius' lips, "Et tu Brute?" – which means "You too Brutus?"

Upon Julius' death, the empire was embroiled in a series of bloodbaths resulting from rivals vying for control. Though Octavius was clearly to be the Successor, he had to fight those who would usurp his ascendancy to the throne. Octavius ascended to undisputed supremacy in 31 B.C. by defeating his last remaining rival, Mark Antony, (lover of the famous Egyptian Queen, Cleopatra) in a military battle at Actium. In 29 B.C. the Roman Senate declared Octavius Rome's first Emperor. Two years later they honored him with the title *Augustus,* which means *exalted one* – a term signifying religious veneration. This signified the beginning of the Roman practice of attributing worship to Caesar as god. With this, Rome's republican government was effectively abolished, and Augustus was given supreme military power. He reigned until his death at age 76 (A.D. 14).

This ushered in what history recognizes as "Pax Romana", or "Roman Peace" throughout the empire. Please don't miss this! Under the providence of God, this marked what the Bible calls "The fullness of time". Galatians 4:4 says, "But when the fullness of time came, God sent forth His Son, born of a woman, born under the Law." This world peace, stable government, the official language – Greek (the language of the New Testament!), and phenomenal worldwide system of Roman highways, facilitated by Pax Romana, under God's providential work, marked the fullness of divine time. In the Greek language, there are two words that translate by our English word *Time*. One is *Kronos,* which is where we get the word *Chronology.* This is *horizontal time.* This is seconds, and minutes, and days, and weeks, and months, and years, and decades, and millennial time. However, the Greek word used in Galatians 4:4 is *Kairos.* This is divinely-intersected time. This is *crises time.* This is the time when God, according to His divine will, intersects *chronological time!* This was the divinely determined time for God to introduce "the seed of the woman", (Genesis 3:15) Jesus Christ, into the world!

The text of Luke, describing the birth of Jesus, identifies the census that was the very first in which the Jews were to be counted by Rome. Previously, only Roman citizens were counted, and that for the purpose of Military Service. However, this particular census marked the first mandate for Jews to be counted, and this was used for the purpose of the levying of poll taxes. The Jews hated this tax, and thus, this census, which was to be taken every 14 years. Is this not the very definition of *Historicity?* (3)

When the Pharisees and Herodians (normally vicious enemies, but a common hatred makes for strange bedfellows) came to try to trap Jesus into a civil dispute with the Roman government, Jesus issued His famous "Show Me the money" statement. Matthew 22:17-21 says, "tell us then, what do You think? Is it lawful to give a poll-tax to Caesar, or not? But Jesus perceived their malice, and said, 'Why are you testing Me, you hypocrites? Show Me the coin used for the poll-tax.' And they brought Him a denarius. And He said to them, 'Whose likeness and inscription is this?' They said to Him, 'Caesar's.' Then He said to them, 'Then render to Caesar the things that are Caesar's; and to God the things that are God's. And hearing this, they were amazed, and leaving Him, they went away." Jesus eluded their attempted trap and rebuked them by asking His question and in giving His answer.

Genesis 1:27 says, "So God created man in His own image, in the image of God created He him: male and female created He them." We are to contribute to the work of the Lord, but He doesn't need your money! His image is stamped on you; So, you are to be totally surrendered to Him! Question: How well are you doing this daily? He wants you, and with your surrender to Him comes all that you *think* you own! Psalm 24:1 says, "The earth is the LORD's and the fullness thereof, the world and those who dwell therein." So, to paraphrase, Jesus said that's Caesar's money, evidenced by his likeness on it, belongs to Caesar. Man belongs to God, evidenced by God's likeness being stamped on him!

> **My house shall be called *of all nations* the house of prayer? But you have made it a den of thieves"**

It is noteworthy that the Jews considered Roman coinage to be heretical because it bore the image of Caesar. In fact, the use of Roman coinage in the temple was expressly forbidden because of this. The leaders of the Temple, the Sadducees, sold sacrificial animals from the Royal Stoa, located next to the Court of the Gentiles. When a Jewish worshipper came to purchase a sacrificial animal, he first had to go to the Temple Money Changers to exchange his Roman Coinage into Jewish currency. These unscrupulous Money Changers robbed the people on the exchange rate. This is why Jesus said that they had turned his house into a "den of thieves" (Luke 19:46).

The Sadducees, who ran the Temple, decided they didn't have enough storage to keep up with the demand for sacrificial animals for sell. They kept the demand skyrocketing by arbitrarily rejecting most sacrificial animals brought to worship by the worshipers! So, they expanded the Royal Stoa by taking space from the Court of the Gentiles. After all, the Court of the Gentiles was exponentially larger than the next largest Court. This is what infuriated Jesus and caused Him to physically drive out the Money Changers and the animals! The Sadducees had created a stumbling block for Gentiles coming to worship God! Want proof? In Mark 11:17 the text says, "And He taught, saying unto them, is it not written, My house shall be called *of all nations* the house of prayer? But you have made it a den of thieves" (emphasis mine). God's intention *always* included Gentiles as those He would save, and the Sadducees had violated that! They had shown total disregard for the will of God in bringing Gentiles to faith in Him!

So, Matthew's gospel account corroborates with Luke's account of the poll-tax decreed by Rome with the implementation of the first Roman census in which the Jews were to be counted. Luke marks the birth of Jesus Christ by the very first Roman census that mandated all Jewish males, 20 years of age and older, had to be counted! We have a gospel whose anchor drags squarely in the mainstream of world history! Luke's account of Jesus' birth is marked by indisputable *Historicity!*

Luke's not finished with this historical time-period stamp on the birth of Christ. In Luke 2:2 he says, "This was the first census taken while Quirinius was governor of Syria." Now fixing a precise date for this census is most difficult. Roman history documents that Publius Sulpicius Quirinius served twice as the Governor of Syria during the period of 6-9 A.D. The ancient Jewish Historian,

Josephus, records that a historically well documented census was taken in Palestine in 6 A.D., and it sparked a violent Jewish revolt. This is mentioned by Luke, quoting Gamaliel, in Acts 5:37 ("After this man, Judas of Galilee rose up in the days of the census and drew away some people after him; he too perished, and those who followed him were scattered.") However, that cannot be the census Luke has in mind here (Luke 2:2) because it occurred about a decade after the death of Herod – much too late to fit Luke's chronology here. So, how do we solve this, apparent, historical discrepancy?

We know that Luke's prowess, as a Historian, was impeccable. How? The famous English Historian, Sir William Ramsey, (as a non-Christian) originally believed that Luke's historical accounts were flawed. So, he undertook a painstakingly thorough investigation of Luke's history. At every point, Luke's history stood, and Sir William Ramsey was bowed a little further. When he finished his investigation, he declared Luke's historical accounts to be unassailable, and he (Ramsey) bowed his knee, in faith, to Jesus Christ and became an avid Believer and follower of the Lord Jesus! But again, how was the (alleged) historical time-period discrepancy rectified? Well, I'm glad you asked!

A fragment of stone discovered at Tivoli (near Rome) in 1764 A.D. contains an inscription in honor of a Roman official who, it states, was "twice governor of Syria and Phoenicia during the reign of Caesar Augustus." The name of the official is not on the fragment, but his accomplishments are there listed. Both Secular, and Christian Historians confirm that these details of this official's accomplishments can fit no other historical Syrian Governor than Publius Sulpicius Quirinus; This confirms historical accounts that Quirinius served twice as the Syrian Governor. From historical records found in Egypt, the world-wide census was ordered in 8 B.C., but wasn't carried out in the region of Palestine until 2-4 years later. Therefore, the precise year of Christ's birth cannot be known with exact certainty; but it was no earlier than 6 B.C., and certainly no later than 4 B.C. Roman history of the Syrian Governor, Quirinius', reign is identified by Luke 2:2! The *Historicity* of the Bible is beautifully without dispute!

Authority of the Bible

What do we mean by *Authority?* Merriam-Webster's gives us the definition. *Authority* - the power or right to give orders, make decisions, and enforce obedience. Example: "He had absolute *authority over* his subordinates". The Bible posits that it, as the very words of God, is absolutely *authoritative.* Both Peter, and John say, "We saw it; We were there"! Peter adds that, in spite of that mountain-top Spiritual experience, we have something that totally *supersedes* that; We have the word of God that is *far more sure* than any experience and you'd do well to take heed of it! This passage, 1 Peter 1:16-20, is a huge indictment on the great segment of Christianity that places personal, esoteric experience and emotions above the very words of God! When their private personal experiences are brought under the light of scripture, I've heard professing Christians say, "Well, I see what that passage seems to be saying, *but I know what happened to me!*"

> ## They put a *devil* in the water and a *wet devil* came out!

My Mother, Sarah Josephine Douglas, a godly woman, is with the Lord. When I was growing up, she pastored a Pentecostal Church in Kentucky. I played guitar, as one of the church musicians. I was a very rebellious child by nature, and I especially rebelled against her being a pastor. In my mind I couldn't reconcile how daddy could be the leader of the home, but momma was the leader of the church. At the time, I didn't know what the scripture said about spiritual leadership in the church, but it just didn't "fit" for me. I had no scriptural understanding; Though I had been water baptized, I was lost. They put a *devil* in the water and a *wet devil* came out! That accurately describes my first water baptism. Many years later, after God had saved me (and I was subsequently validly baptized) and placed men in my life to intentionally disciple me, I would have Biblical discussions with my mom when I would visit her. It was not uncommon for our Biblical discussions, at her dining room table with open Bibles, to last all night. I look back on those memories with much thankfulness to our Lord; How many men can say they had multiple opportunities to sit and discuss, and reason with their mom from the scriptures all night long?

On one such occasion, our discussion and study centered around whether the Bible supported the existence of women pastors and preachers. You can imagine that we didn't just happen upon the topic; I had studied the matter very deeply for many years, and was prepared and praying, for the right time, to offer her the light that the Lord had given me upon it.

One of the key passages (and there are many) we examined was from the *Pastoral* epistle in 1 Timothy 3:1-7 which says, "It is a trustworthy statement: if any man aspires to the office of overseer, it is a fine work he desires to do. An overseer, then, must be above reproach, the husband of one wife, temperate, prudent, respectable, hospitable, able to teach, not addicted to wine or pugnacious, but gentle, peaceable, free from the love of money. He must be one who manages his own household well, keeping his children under control with all dignity (but if a man does not know how to manage his own household, how will he take care of the church of God?), and not a new convert, so that he will not become conceited and fall into the condemnation incurred by the devil. And he must have a good reputation with those outside the church so that he will not fall into reproach and the snare of the devil."

I explained that, beginning in 1 Timothy 2:8 through 3:7, God laid down the qualifications for being a Pastor, Elder, or Bishop, which are equivalent terms in the original language of the Bible. I explained all of the Greek *masculine* pronouns in the passage, and then zeroed in on one particular qualification – the one that dictates that *he* must be *"the husband of one wife..."* In Greek it literally says that he must be a *"one-woman man"*. The issue is not the Elder's marital status, but his moral and sexual purity. I explained how some interpret this to be a prohibition against polygamy – an unnecessary injunction since polygamy was not common in Roman society, and clearly forbidden by scriptures (see Genesis 2:24; Matthew 19:5,6; Mark 10:6-9, Ephesians 5:31).

Now, some would argue that the Patriarchs had multiple wives. That is true, but it was not sanctioned by God; It was, in fact, diametrically opposed to God's clear marriage prescription found in Genesis 2:24. Others see this requirement as barring those who remarried after the death of their wives, but the issue is purity not marital status. Some posit that Paul, here, excludes divorced men from church leadership. That, again, ignores the fact that this qualification does not deal with marital status. Nor does the Bible prohibit all remarriage after divorce. Yet others see it as a requirement for the Elder/Pastor to be married; Again, the issue has nothing to do with marital status. Further, if that were true, Paul himself would've been disqualified. 1 Corinthians 7:8 says, "For I would that all men were even as I myself. But every man hath his proper gift of God, one after this manner, and another after that." Paul confirms that he was given the gift of *celibacy,* and he's confirming that everyone doesn't possess that gift! A "one-woman man" is one totally devoted to his wife, or if single, one who is not a *womanizer.* Then, I pointed out that *no woman could possibly meet this qualification and therefore all women are disqualified, according to God's standard, as Pastors/Elders.* In fact, God's primary messengers have always been male, and that includes angels. The Bible teaches us those angels are God's divine

41

messengers. In the original biblical languages, every time the word translated *angel* appears it is always a *masculine noun.* Anytime the Bible gives us the name of the angel bringing God's message that angel always appears as a man. Despite the biblical error portrayed by many Christian artists, there is no such thing as a female angel! God is not politically correct, and neither is the divine structure of His Church! There was total silence at the table for several minutes while mom pondered this exposition of scripture. After a very long pause, she said, *"I hear what you're saying."* I interrupted her and said, *"It doesn't matter what I say. Do you see what the very words of God say?"* Her classic reply is forever burned into my memory. She said, *"I see what this seems to be saying, but I know what happened to me. I know that God called me to preach, and I won't take down for anybody!"* Respectfully, I closed this all-night discussion with these words. "Psalm 138:2 says, I will worship toward your holy temple, and praise your name for your lovingkindness and for your truth; for *you has magnified your word above your name"* (emphasis mine). God holds His word above His very name – the name that is above all names – so how, in the name of heaven, can any professing Christian elevate esoteric experience and emotion above the truth set forth in the word of God?" *Truth* is only what God says! In the Body of Christ at large, is there *vast* room for *repentance* at this point? 4

Sister Sarah Josephine Douglas was not only my mom, she was also at the very top of the list of all the counselors, confidantes, and friends I've had in life. From my earliest childhood, she taught me that, no matter what she was doing, no matter the time of day, nor the darkest night, no matter the topic of concern, I had cart blanc access to her for any discussion.

We lived this to the fullest extent. Many of my childhood friends have been shocked and embarrassed when, in the types of discussions young boys always have, about relationships, sex, etc., I would quickly go into the next room and ask my mom for the answer! My Mom and I would, alternately, call and sing to one another on our respective birthdays. For years I'd sing to her the song, "Mama" produced by Boyz to Men, or "Mama Knew Love" produced by Anthony Hamilton.

Such was my relationship with my mom. During the last three weeks of her life, she lived with my eldest Sister, Wanda Veney, a career professional in Elderly and Hospice Care. My wife, Amy, and I basically moved in with Wanda, her husband, Jonathan, and my niece, Armenthia, in Virginia, so that we could help care for Mom and enjoy what would be the end of our earthly fellowship. As she lay dying from kidney failure, I sat with her, day and night, reminiscing and laughing about our lives together, reading scripture to her, and serenading her by singing and playing guitar. The scripture that seemed to bring her the most comfort was the same one that brought comfort to my father as he "walked through the valley of the shadow of death" back in 1982.

Psalm 121:1-4 says, "I will lift up my eyes to the mountains; From where shall my help come from? My help comes from the LORD, who made heaven and earth. He will not allow your foot to slip; He Who keeps you will not slumber. Behold He Who keeps Israel will neither slumber nor sleep. The LORD is your keeper; The LORD is your shade on your right hand. The sun will not smite you by day, nor the moon by night. The LORD will protect you from all evil; He will keep your soul. The LORD will guard your going out and your coming in from this time forth and forever."

Two of the songs that she seemed to enjoy most were "It Is Well with My Soul", by Horatio Spafford, along with my rendition of "Sarah Smile", produced by Daryl Hall and John Oates. The day that God took her home, I remember my greatest sense of loss was that of the expressions of love, fellowship, and camaraderie we had shared for a lifetime; I also remember the sense of joy and comfort in knowing that, at God's appointed time, we would resume our fellowship – this time for eternity. We loved each other to the maximum, though we disagreed on several doctrinal issues.

The Bible is the nature and character of God in black and white. That's not the worship of a book, but rather, it is the worship of the One Who authored the book. 2 Timothy 3:16-17 says, "All scripture is inspired by God and profitable for teaching, for reproof, for correction, for training in righteousness; so that the man of God may be adequate, equipped for every good work." The Greek word

44

translated "inspired by God" is the Greek word *theopneustos;*
Theo=God. Pneuma is the Greek root for *spirit, air, wind, or breath.*
It literally means "divinely breathed". The Holy Spirit, the third
member of the Trinity, is described throughout the Bible as the
"breath of God." On *Shavuot,* the God-ordained Jewish Feast that
we Christians call *Pentecost,* Acts 2:2 says, "And suddenly there
came from heaven a noise like a violent rushing *wind,* and it filled
the whole house where they were sitting…" This was the official
coming of the Holy Spirit to permanently indwell each believer to
unite us to Christ and to each other as members of His Body. The
aforementioned text, 2 Timothy 3:16-17, tells us that this same Holy
Spirit of God authored the Bible. So, all scripture was authored by
the Holy Spirit of God. In all of the universe there is no higher
authority!

Psalm 19 and Psalm 119, give the greatest commentary in scripture
on the very words of God. Psalm 19:7-11 is replete   in its
descriptions of the authority, and effectiveness of the word of God.
It says, "The *Law* of the LORD is *perfect,* restoring the soul; The
Testimony of the LORD is *sure,* making wise the simple. The
Precepts of the LORD are *right,* rejoicing the heart; The
Commandment of the LORD is *pure,* enlightening the eyes. The
Fear of the LORD is *clean,* enduring forever; The *Judgments* of the
LORD are *true*; they are righteous altogether. They are more
desirable than gold, yes, than much fine gold; sweeter also than
honey and the drippings of the honeycomb. Moreover, by them
Your servant is warned; In keeping them there is great reward."
Here we see six titles for the word of God, six massive attributes of
the word of God, and six overwhelming benefits of studying and
applying the word of God in the human life!

Psalm 119:9 says, "How shall a young man cleanse his way? By
taking heed thereto according to your word." Finally, there is the
prayer of the Psalmist for illumination upon the word of God. Psalm

119:18 says, "Open my eyes that I may behold wondrous things out of Your law." We don't get to pick and choose which passages of the Bible we wish to honor and obey, though many have tried. For example, Thomas Jefferson wrote his own personal version of the Bible! No! Either, it is *all* authoritative or *none* of it is authoritative! The Bible is supremely authoritative in that it is the only official, God-breathed, repository where the very words of the God of the universe can be found!

Authenticity of the Bible

No doubt, you've heard the popular academic argument against the *authenticity* of scripture that says, "Well, actually the Bible has been translated so many times, and what they have done during those translations is a lot of redactions in order to make events and stories harmonize. Therefore, what we have is not what *really* happened, but we have what was written by the *later* community."

Well, who is the *later community?* Who were these *overzealous scribes, or Monks,* that have labored diligently to change things so they harmonize and corroborate? This would've been an untenable task for these *imaginary scribes,* or *overzealous Monks.* If they were going to change the Bible, by *doctoring* the original manuscripts, they would have had huge problems; They would've had three insurmountable problems in particular.

First, they would have had a manuscript problem, because when we consider the New Testament, alone, they would have had to locate 6000 manuscripts, or portions of manuscripts. A *manuscript* is a handwritten composition on paper, bark, cloth, metal, palm leaf or any other material dating back at least seventy-five years that has significant scientific, *historical* or aesthetic value. Lithographs and printed volumes are not *manuscripts. Manuscripts* have knowledge content.1   These *hypothetical Monks* would've had to change all 6000 manuscripts, the exact same way, and not allow their alterations to show. Then, they would've had to get them back to where they stole them from without being discovered, and they would've had to execute the theft, the tedious time-consuming task of making the changes, and the return of these documents before anyone noticed that they had been missing. ₁

Well, in this endeavor, we're only considering 6000 manuscripts; Would this be a big deal? Surely not...right? Let's compare the body of evidence, the manuscripts, for the Bible to some other ancient, famous, historically, authentically, and universally accepted, literary works. There are fewer than 10 manuscripts of Homer's *Herodotus*. There are only 5 manuscripts of *Aristotle's Poetics*. There are only 10 manuscripts of Julius Caesar's *Gallic Wars*. However, we have 6000 manuscripts of the New Testament!

One of the guidelines for evaluating the *authenticity* of a literary work is that you must consider how long after the historic event the first formal documentation appeared describing that event. Let's consider this relative to the Bible, as well as the literary works cited above. We have New Testament manuscripts, or portions of manuscripts, that date back as early as AD 120 to 150. Critics of Biblical *authenticity* say, "That's a long time after the events described." Really? Julius Caesar's *Gallic Wars* was written about 900 years after the events described. Aristotle's *Poetics* were published about 1300 years after the events described. Homer's *Herodotus* appeared about 2100 years after the events described. So, after 100's of years Historical and Literary Critics accepts accounts of these events. Compare that with this: *The New Testament was written within the actual lifetime of eye witnesses!*

Next, Peter says the Bible reports *supernatural events*. *"For when He received honor and glory from God the Father, such an utterance as this was made to Him by the Majestic Glory, "This is My Beloved Son with whom I am well-pleased"—and we ourselves heard this utterance made from heaven when we were with Him on the holy mountain.*" These are not just things that are happening out of the ordinary. These are *supernatural* events, such as, a shriveled, atrophied hand being instantly made as healthy as the other hand (Mark 3:3-5). Then, there was the man who was born blind instantly receiving his sight (John 9:1-11). Next, there's the recording of a paralytic, who had never walked in his life, being told to raise up and take his pallet and walk (John 5:5-9). Additionally, the Bible reports that Jesus sent His Disciples across the lake in a boat, and while they're rowing and striving against a great storm, He comes walking to them on the water (Mark 6:45-51)!

This reminds me of a story about Billy Martin, the famous former coach of the New York Yankees baseball team. As the story goes, the Yankees had signed a new ace pitcher who reported to Martin for orientation. They discussed several team rules, and finally Martin advised the player that He could no longer wear shoulder-length hair and he needed an immediate haircut. The player responded that "Jesus had long hair and that didn't hamper Him." The coach got up from his desk, walked over and opened a set of French doors revealing an Olympic-sized swimming pool. The coach then pointed to the pool and said, "Go ahead. Walk across that and you may grow your hair as long as you like! Otherwise, show up tomorrow with a haircut!"

Next, let us consider the well-rehearsed story of Jesus raising Lazarus from the dead. John 11:6 tells us that when Jesus heard that Lazarus was sick, He "then stayed two days longer in the place where He was." It is as if Jesus wanted to make certain that Lazarus was dead before He arrived! I'm not manufacturing this. In John 11:14 we read, "So Jesus then said to them plainly, Lazarus is dead, and I am glad for your sakes that I was not there, so that you may believe; but let us go to him." This flies in the face of the *health, wealth, and prosperity preachers that say, "God wants all Christians healthy, wealthy and prosperous."* No! Sometimes God wants a Christian sick, and sometimes He wants a Christian dead! However, we'll not stop here.

In John 11:23 Jesus told Martha, sister of Lazarus, "Your brother will rise again." Martha responded, "I know that he will rise again in the resurrection on the last day." To this Jesus responded, "I am the resurrection and the life: he who believes in Me will live even If he dies..." This is one of eight *I am* statements included in John's gospel. Here, Jesus equated Himself to God the Father, taking the holy name that God revealed to Moses in the burning bush incident of Exodus 3:14. In Exodus 3:13-14 we read, "Then Moses said to God, Behold, I am going to the sons of Israel, and I will say to them, The God of your fathers has sent me to you. Now they may say to me, What Is His name? What shall I say to them? God said to Moses, I AM Who I Am; and He said thus you shall say to the sons of Israel *I Am* has sent me to you." This name of God was considered so holy that the people of Jesus' day would not even utter it out loud! Jesus used this name for Himself every time He declared the words *I Am*. We know that the Jews understood this as His claim to be God; they sought to kill Him when He used this name.

Continuing with the story of the raising of Lazarus from the dead, consider John 11:39. Jesus said, "Remove the stone. Martha, the sister of the deceased, said to Him, Lord, by this time there will be a stench, for he has been dead four days." Or...in perfect *King James English, "Lord, by now he stinketh!"* Pick up the reading at John 11:41-44. "So, they removed the stone. Then Jesus raised His eyes, and said, Father I thank You that You have heard Me. I knew that You always hear Me; but because of the people standing around I said It, so that they may believe that You sent Me." When He had said these things He cried out with a loud voice, Lazarus come forth. The man who had died came forth, bound hand and foot with wrappings, and his face was wrapped around with a cloth. Jesus said to them, unbind him, and let him go."

> **Before Jesus saves a person, that person is a *dead man walking!***

Other than the feeding of the five thousand, this is one of Jesus' most famous and most talked about miracles. This man had been dead for four days, and was in an advanced state of decomposition, and Jesus spoke the words and brought him back to life! The scriptures record that Jesus raised three people from the dead. Jarius' daughter had just died and Jesus raised her from the dead. The son of the widow at Nain had been dead two days (because the Jews bury on the second day) and Jesus raised him from the dead. Here, He raised Lazarus from the dead. All three of these people were dead. However, they were in different stages of corruption. When Jesus raised people from the dead the Holy Spirit is giving us a picture of *salvation.* Ephesians 2:1-2 describes our pre-salvation condition. "And you were dead in your trespasses and sins, in which you formerly walked according to the course of this world, according to the prince of the power of the air, of the spirit that is now working in the sons of disobedience." Before Jesus saves a person, that person is a *dead man walking!*

Since Lazarus was dead, what did he contribute to the process of being brought back to life? Nothing! A dead man can't contribute. He can't even contribute to his decomposition; that happens *to him.* Lazarus had lungs and no air. He had a heart that pumped no blood. There was oxygen located in the tomb. Everything required for life was in the tomb except the very words of God! Question: When Jesus said, "Lazarus, come forth", did a dead man hear his name? Be very careful with my question; hearing is a sign of life! Let's let the Bible answer.

Consider Ezekiel 2:1-2, where we read, "Then He said to me, Son of man, stand on your feet that I may speak with you! As He spoke to me the Spirit entered me and set me on my feet, and I heard Him speaking to me." Implied here is an inability of Ezekiel to stand on his feet. He said that as God spoke to him the Spirit entered him and set him upon his feet. So (don't miss this) communicated *in* the command of God was the *ability* to respond! Remember, Lazarus being physically dead is a picture of people (before salvation) being spiritually dead. When Jesus called Lazarus forth, in that command was communicated the ability to respond! Now, someone will say, "Yeah, he raised me from the dead (Spiritually), but *I* had to exercise *faith.*" That's not correct per Ephesians 2:8-9, where we read, "By grace are you saved through faith, and that not of yourselves. It is the gift of God, not of works, lest any man should boast." *Grace* is unmerited favor. The text says we're saved by *grace* through *faith.* Then, the text says, and that (the faith) not of yourselves. *IT* (the antecedent for the faith) *is the gift of God.* This passage clearly tells us that the *faith* is part of the salvation package that God gives! Accordingly, just as the raising of four-days-dead Lazarus was a supernatural feat, so is the miracle of salvation every time Jesus saves a person!

Do you remember our initial statement of why we can trust the Bible? *"The Bible is a reliable collection of historical documents written down by eye witnesses during the lifetime of other eye witnesses. They report to us supernatural events that took place in fulfillment of specific prophecies and claim to be divine rather than human in origin."* The truth of the supernatural events of the Bible gets even better and more glorious!

Finally, the Bible reports on the most monumental, earth-shattering, God-satisfying event in the history of the universe; That would be the crucifixion and death of Jesus on Friday (John 19:30), and His resurrection from the dead-on Sunday (Matthew 28:6)! This is the greatest, most efficacious, most widely-proclaimed supernatural event the world has ever known! These are the types of supernatural events that the Bible records, and these events took place in fulfillment of specific prophecies – some of which were written more than a century (in the Bible) before their occurrence!

For example, Psalm 22 gives, what is considered, the most detailed account of the crucifixion of Christ in all of the Bible – including the gospels! Psalm 22:1 says, "My God, my God, why have You forsaken me?" These are the very words of Jesus spoken from the cross! Psalm 22:16 says, "They pierced my hands and my feet." This is the very thing that happened to Jesus on the cross, and it was written, at least, 750 years before Jesus arrived at Bethlehem; Further, it was written by a writer in a culture that (at the time of the writing) knew absolutely *nothing* about crucifixion! The fulfillment of these prophecies, and many, many, others authenticate the Bible.

The oldest prophecy given to man is found in Genesis 3:15. It is a prophecy of the birth, death, and resurrection of our Lord Jesus Christ! These supernatural events unequivocally substantiate the truth of the authenticity of the Bible.

First Gospel, Isaiah

Another example of the authenticity of the Bible is found in Isaiah 53. You must understand its character and context so that you may be able to grasp the height, depth, and breadth of this monumental chapter. Now, the context of this passage actually begins in chapter 52:13, so any study of Isaiah chapter 53 must begin there. Nearly all Christians are familiar with this passage. However, it has been my experience that we usually know the least about those passages of scripture that are most familiar to us! That is true of passages such as Psalm 23, Luke 15, John 15, John 3:16, and it is also true of Isaiah 53.

Many Reformation and Puritan era scholars have referred to Isaiah 53 as the "The Fifth Gospel", in relation to Matthew, Mark, Luke, and John. However, chronologically, it should be considered the *First Gospel!* Aurelius Augustine, of Hippo, said, "It is not a prophecy, it is a gospel." One of the early church fathers was Polycarp. He was a disciple of the Apostle John. He lived from AD 69-155, and was stabbed to death; This was after being burned at the stake when the fire failed to consume his body! Polycarp called Isaiah 53 "The Golden Passional of the Old Testament." The "Father of the Reformation", Martin Luther, said, "Every Christian ought to be able to repeat it (Isaiah 53) by heart."

Isaiah is a *microcosm* of the entire Bible. Isaiah has 66 chapters; The Bible has 66 books. Isaiah is divided into two sections. Chapters 1 through 39 make up the first section, and chapters 40 through 66 make up the second section. The first 39 chapters of Isaiah deal with *pronouncement of judgement on Israel*; The final 27 chapters deal with Israel's deliverance from captivity and (end times) *eschatological Kingdom salvation.* The first 39 books of the Bible deal with Law and judgement; The final 27 books, the New Testament, deal with grace, salvation, and eschatological Kingdom salvation. The final 27 chapters of Isaiah are broken into 3 segments of 9 chapters each. The first segment of 9 chapters, 40-48, has to do with Israel's salvation from Babylon; The last segment of 9 chapters, 58-66, has to do with the eschatological kingdom salvation to come. The middle segment of 9 chapters, 49-57, has to do with *salvation from sin* for the people of God, both, Jew and Gentile. This salvation from sin, for Jew and Gentile, is going to come through the Servant of Jehovah, who will be the Messiah (Jesus) sent from God.

The middle of the segment of 9 chapters is 49-57 are 52 and 53. The middle verse of this middle segment is 53:5, "He was pierced through for our transgressions, He was crushed for our iniquities, the chastening for our wellbeing fell on Him and by His scourging we are healed." Middle section, middle chapters, middle of the chapter, middle verse. The Holy Spirit (the author of the Bible) funnels the entire Biblical narrative from God's "Thesis Statement" (found in

Genesis 3:15) down to the substitutionary piercing of the Servant of Jehovah – the Lord Jesus Christ! This is where Genesis 3:15 reaches fulfillment; The 'seed of the woman crushed the head of the seed of the serpent'!

Since we have now spoken of the basic layout of the book it is important that we look at the prophetic nature and what it tells us. Isaiah is considered to be one of the "Major Prophets", as opposed to being one of the "Minor Prophets". The "Major Prophet" designation has nothing to with being *greater,* but rather is so designated due to the *length* of the prophecy given through the writer. Isaiah was written at least 750 years before Christ came into His creation at Bethlehem. The first half of the book, chapters 1 through 39, speak of coming judgment and captivity of Israel. That prophecy was virtually, immediately, fulfilled when David's southern kingdom, Judah, went into captivity. Chapter 39 ends with a pronunciation of the judgment that's going to come on Israel in the Babylonian captivity. In Isaiah 39 verses 6 and 7 we read, "The days are coming when all that is in your house and all that your fathers have laid up in store to this day will be carried to Babylon. Nothing will be left, says the Lord, and some of your sons who will issue from you whom you will beget will be taken away and they will become officials in the palace of the King of Babylon." This is a prophecy about the Babylonian captivity, which began approximately 80 years after Isaiah wrote it! So, the book of Isaiah authenticates the Bible, and its historicity *and* veracity are confirmed, as both Biblical and *Secular* history document fulfillment of this very prophecy!

It is fascinating that the second half of Isaiah's prophecy, chapters 40 to 66, begins where the New Testament begins. In Isaiah chapter 40:1 we read, "Comfort, O comfort My people, says your God. Speak kindly to Jerusalem." This is the point where God turns from pronouncing judgment on Israel, to pronouncing grace and salvation upon them. Here, in chapter 40:3, we have the prophecy about John the Baptist. As we know, John was "A voice is calling, clear the way for the Lord in the wilderness, make smooth in the desert a highway for our God." The New Testament gospels confirm this. In John 1:23, in response to the question concerning who he was, John the Baptist responded, "I am a voice of one crying out in the wilderness: Prepare the way for the Lord: Make straight the way of the Lord – just as Isaiah the prophet said." John the Baptist, as the forerunner of Christ, was the fulfillment of Isaiah's prophecy. So, the New Testament begins exactly where the second half (the final 27 chapters) of Isaiah begins!

Next, the New Testament ends where the second half of Isaiah ends. Isaiah 65:17 says this, "For behold, I create new heavens and a new earth." Then in chapter 66 verse 22, we read, "For just as the new heavens and the new earth which I make will endure before Me, declares the Lord…". How does the New Testament end? It ends in Revelation 21 and 22 with the new heavens and the new earth. So, this section of Isaiah (chapters 40-66) begins where the New Testament begins, with the arrival of John the Baptist, and it ends where the New Testament ends, with the new heaven and the new earth. All of this was written 750 years before "the seed of the woman," Jesus, enters His creation to begin to fulfill, not only Isaiah's prophecy, but the first prophecy God gave to man in Genesis 3:15 – God's *Thesis Statement* of the Bible! The culmination of God's *Thesis Statement* is recorded in the book of Revelation with the eternal spending of God's wrath on all of those who have rejected the salvation wrought by the work of 'the seed of the woman'. The book of Revelation ends with the marriage supper of the 'Lamb of God' (the seed of the woman – Jesus Christ) to His bride, the church, made up of all redeemed sinners from all ages! Eternal life in the *new heavens and new earth* becomes permanent at that time!

The *authenticity* of the Bible is seen in the fact that secular and biblical history, both, document the fulfillment of many of the prophecies contained in this passage! It is further validated in that every prophecy the Bible has given consistently comes to fruition; That includes the one given 1500 years before it's fulfillment when the 'seed of the woman' crushed the serpent's head on the cross! Hebrews 2:14 says, "Forasmuch then as the children are partakers of flesh and blood, He also Himself likewise took part of the same; that through death He might destroy him that had the power of death, that is, the devil…" The *authenticity* of the Bible has been, and continues to be, validated by fulfilled prophecies.

Veracity of the Bible

The most common argument against the *veracity*, of the Bible is one that I'm certain you've heard multiple times. "Men wrote the Bible, so you can't trust it. You can't trust anything that men have had a hand in!" The Oxford Dictionary defines *veracity* as "Conformity to the facts; Accuracy; Truthfulness. Example: "Voters should be concerned about his *veracity* and character."

So how is the *veracity* of the Bible established? 2 Peter 1:21 says, "…for no prophecy was ever made by an act of human will, but men moved by the Holy Spirit spoke from God." The word *moved* (in Greek it's *pheromenoi*) is a present, passive, participle that literally means "carried along". So, the will, vocabulary, syntax, and grammar of the writers of scripture were *carried along* by the Holy Spirit of God!

Let me illustrate. In grade school, you most likely played this game. The teacher would quietly, privately, whisper a sentence into the ear of one of the students. That student was to quietly, privately whisper the *exact* sentence into the ear of a fellow student. This process would continue throughout the class. The last student to receive the sentence would then recite it, aloud, to the class, and it was amazing how little that recitation resembled the sentence that the teacher initially whispered to the first student! However, there is only one way the teacher may have assured the integrity of the sentence passed from student to student; She would need to personally superintend each passing (carrying along) of the sentence from student to student! This is a crude example of how the Holy Spirit authored scripture. He personally breathed the words, the vocabulary, syntax, and grammar into the heart, mind, will, and pen of each writer. This is not simply a book written by multiple human authors! The Bible is the inspired word of God authored by the Holy Spirit of God!

Next, no doubt, you've heard this argument. "I'll believe the Bible if you can prove it scientifically!" Well, that presents a very serious problem. One who would make such a statement indicates that he/she is ill-equipped for a proper discussion of this. Further, such a statement indicates a couple of other things. *Number one*, this person has no clue about the historicity, authority, and authenticity of the Bible. *Number two*, this person knows nothing about the scientific method of proof. In order to employ the *scientific method* of proof, something has to be observable, measurable and repeatable. Do you immediately see the problem here? Historical events aren't demonstrable, measurable, nor repeatable. One can't use the *scientific method* to prove that Abe Lincoln was ever President of these United States! So, if you actually have a problem with the Bible because you can't apply the scientific method of proof, you have a problem with proving history in general, because no historical fact can be proven using the *Scientific method of proof!*

The Bible is completely without scientific error; However, the Bible is not a *scientific* book. It is a *historical* book. For a historical document, one must employ the *Evidentiary Method* of proof for determining *veracity*. Historically, if something is written, the only way you can question it is if you don't have *corroboration*, or if there is internal inconsistency. We can't find any internal inconsistency in the Bible in its original form, and we have a plethora of corroboration. The Bible contains four languages, Greek, Hebrew, Aramaic and Chaldean (Daniel). The Bible's setting takes place on three continents, Asia, Africa and Europe. The Bible was written by 40 authors, most of whom never met one another, because they wrote over a period of some 1600 years. Look in your Webster's Dictionary; That would be the very definition of corroboration. Webster's says, "Corroboration is the ability to compare information provided by two separate sources and find similarities between them. When a second source provides the same or similar information to the first, the second source is considered to corroborate (e.g., support, or agree with) with the first. Finding corroboration between sources strengthens your conclusions, especially when you are making a historical argument."

To date, though many have tried, no one has produced any evidentiary information that would negate what we find in the Bible. Accordingly, the fact must be accepted, based on the *evidentiary method, not the scientific method*, that the Bible is "a reliable collection of historical documents written down by eyewitnesses during the lifetime of other eyewitnesses. They report to us supernatural events that took place in fulfillment of specific prophecies and claim that their writings are divine rather than human in origin."

> **The Bible is absolute *Truth*, as it consists of the very words of God!**

Accordingly, the Bible, in its original manuscript form, contains the very words of God without error; So, the Bible is absolute *Truth,* as it consists of the very words of God! If there is a question in one's mind about whether the Bible is consistent throughout, it is not because of what's written in scripture. It is because of one's limited understanding, education, or study. The Bible, in its original text, represents the very epitome of *Veracity!*

In conclusion, 2 Peter 1:16-20 gives us a replete example of why we can believe the Bible based on the *Evidentiary Method* of determining *Truth.* The Evidentiary Method must include all four of the components that we've expounded. They are: Historicity, Authority, Authenticity, and Veracity. Through application of this universally recognized multi-criteria decision analysis (MCDA) we have established why we can believe the Bible to be true.

Chapter 3 Hindrances to Knowing and Accepting Truth

Hindrances for Unbelievers

There are several hindrances to knowing and accepting Truth. Of course, the enemies of men's souls, Satan and his minions, have been blowing at and trying to extinguish the flame of scripture light since man's creation, without success.

Man's inherent, rebellious, attitude and refusal to accept authority is another factor. The hope of the atheist and the hypocrite is that he will be judged on the basis of something other than Truth; Remember, *truth* is what God says!

Yet another hindrance to knowing and accepting *truth* is being *unregenerate*, or not saved. 1 Corinthians 2:14, in speaking about why the lost man can't receive truth says, "But the natural man receives not the things of the Spirit of God: for they are foolishness to him; neither can he know them, because they are spiritually discerned."

Still another impediment to knowing and accepting *truth* is man's desire to paint a complimentary picture of himself. You see, secular social science teaches that the vast majority of human beings are basically *good*. This premise is based on the fact that few humans are as *bad* as we are inherently capable of being. The teachers and proponents of the social sciences contend that when an Adolf Hitler, or Jeffery Dahmer, or Osama Bin Laden, appears among us it is an aberration. Unfortunately, much contemporary preaching and teaching has subtly indoctrinated the church with this secular worldview. Texts such as Jeremiah 17:9 very rarely receive mention, let alone exposition. Why? It says, "The heart is more deceitful than all else and desperately wicked; Who can understand it?" Now when the Bible speaks of the heart of man it is not referencing that muscle in the center of the chest that pumps blood. That muscle doesn't desire anything, it doesn't know anything, it doesn't emotionally feel anything, and it doesn't control anything beyond the circulatory system! No, when the Bible speaks of the heart of man it is referencing an aspect of the mind. It is speaking of the *seat of thinking*. Proverbs 23:7 says, "For as a man thinks in his heart, so is he..." We all know that man thinks with his mind and not with that muscle in the center of the chest that pumps blood. Accordingly, when the Jeremiah emphatically claims that the heart of man is *more deceitful than all else and is desperately wicked,* he is referencing the seat of thinking – the very core of man!

Our Creator, the God of the Bible presents the truth that is juxtaposed to the worldview of social science, and sadly, much of the church. Today we are realizing the fulfillment of the prophecy of Paul when he wrote these words to his primary disciple, Timothy, in 2 Timothy 4:3,4. It says, "For the time will come when they will not endure sound doctrine; but wanting to have their ears tickled, they will accumulate for themselves teachers in accordance to their own desires, and will turn away their ears from the truth and will turn aside to myths." This is a problem of epidemic proportion in the contemporary church! The more the preacher "tickles the ears" the larger the congregation!

Hindrances for Believers

We now want to give treatment to the biblical reasons why professing Christians have hindrances and resistances to knowing and accepting *Truth*.

As believers in, and followers of, the Lord Jesus Christ, we are to be on a perpetual quest for His truth. Through Peter, in 1 Peter 2:2, the Holy Spirit wrote, "Like newborn babies, long for the pure milk of the word, so that by it you may grow in respect to salvation." We are to hunger and thirst for the very words of God with the same passion, demand, and relentlessness with which a newborn baby pursues milk! When that newborn baby wants milk, there will be no peace for anybody in the household until that burning, yearning, dominate, desire is satisfied. This desire, this demand, is biologically natural to the newborn baby. Now, the same is true about the one who has been born *"anothen"*, which is Greek for "from above". In John 3:3 Jesus said to Nicodemus, "You must be born *'anothen'.*" That word is typically, validly, translated "again". However, as you can see from the Greek rendering, it is much bigger than that! So, just as the biological newborn comes into the world with that natural, burning, hunger for milk, so it is with the one who is Spiritually born 'from above'.

> **If you are a professing Christian and you do not have that burning desire for the very words of God, to the same degree that a biological newborn has for milk, you should critically examine whether you've ever been truly born from above!**

Please give crucial, critical, somber heed to my next statement. If you are a professing Christian and you do not have that burning desire for the very words of God, to the same degree that a biological newborn has for milk, you should critically examine whether you've ever been truly born from above! 2 Corinthians 13:5 commands us to do this. It says, "Test yourselves to see if you are in the faith; examine yourselves! Or do you not recognize this about yourselves, that Jesus Christ is in you-unless indeed you fail the test?" Nothing is more crucial than this. I don't want you to miss this, nor do I want this to miss you. The biological newborn's insatiable desire for milk is immediate and daily. The same is true for the one who has been Spiritually born from above. They should have that same immediate, daily, desire, hunger, craving, for the word of God.

Now, what is 'milk'? Milk is solid food that has been processed through a more mature digestive system. You see, a newborn's digestive system is not mature enough to handle solid food. So that solid food has to be processed to allow that baby digestive system to handle it. As that baby grows, you introduce it, little by little, to solid food. You must begin by placing small bits of solid food on the baby's tongue to stimulate the hunger. Once that child has been on solid food long enough their intake of milk will likely diminish, but the desire now turns to solid food. The same is true of the genuine Christian. Just like that biological baby, the Spiritual baby must be fed with the milk of the word of God. As that Christian grows, he/she is introduced to stronger Spiritual food when a Discipler places small bits of solid food on the baby Christian's *Spiritual tongue* to stimulate the hunger. As this happens, their appetite for milk will be diminished, but their appetite for solid food grows. That's why 1 Peter 2:2 uses the analogy to highlight the *desire* and *not* the milk!

Sadly, unfortunately, many Christians never progress past the milk stage of growth, and that's God's biggest problem. You see, *Satan* is not God's biggest problem; In the divine progression of Genesis 3:15, God defeated him at the cross! No, God's biggest problem is the Christian that stubbornly, willfully refuses to grow in their knowledge, acceptance, and application of truth! I'll explain.

Chapter 4 The Willfully Immature Christian

Those Christians who stubbornly, willfully refuse to grow in the knowledge, acceptance, and application of divine truth do not just show up that way. How they got that way requires a detailed explanation. 1 Corinthians 3:1-4 says, "And I, brethren, could not speak to you as to spiritual men, but as to men of flesh, as to infants in Christ. I gave you milk to drink, not solid food; for you were not yet able to receive it. Indeed, even now you are not yet able, for you are still fleshly. For since there is jealousy and strife among you, are you not fleshly, and are you not walking like mere men?" Those who believe that there's no such thing as a *Willfully Immature Christian,* which is commonly called a *Carnal Christian,* do not fully understand this passage. In verse 1, Paul reminds these Believers that, when he first came to Corinth and led them to Christ, they were "infants in Christ". He said that they were men of flesh at that time. The Greek word for *flesh,* here, is *Sarkikos.* The suffix *ikos* means adapted to, or described by, whatever the first part of the word means. *Sark* is the Greek word for *flesh.* It means to be *constitutionally fleshly.*

These were newborn, baby, Christians that hadn't built up any Spiritual resources because they had just been born from above. They couldn't help but be fleshly! Just like biological newborn babies, their behavior was erratic and puzzling at times! An infant will chew on his hand one minute, and then chew on his foot the next, and doesn't know that either belongs to him! A biological newborn is totally dependent upon someone else to feed, diaper, wash, correct, love, teach, and model these disciplines for him. The same is true with the newborn Christian, and this is the model of *discipling* we see in scripture. Unfortunately, this process is non-existent, or is sorely lacking, in the typical church.

In the typical, institutional church, when a person is born from above, we stand him up front and shout hallelujah around him. Then, when the worship service ends, we "may" hand him a Bible, and sign him up for 'new members class' (which teaches him to give and be a good Baptist, Presbyterian, Methodist, or whatever, and about tithing). Then we tell him we'll see him next week and thrust him out to survive on his own until then! You wouldn't dream of setting the biological newborn out on the doorstep and telling him that you'll see him next week! No, you immediately start to care for that biological newborn. You immediately begin to shower him with love, feed him, change his diaper, train him in behavior, and teach him to feed himself! The exact same care is just as absolutely crucial for the newborn, baby, Christian! We somehow have in our minds that discipling will happen through preaching. This absolutely cannot be done by preaching. Jesus didn't do it that way, so if we do it that way, we will improve upon Him! We act as if somehow the baby Christian is to grow and develop Spiritual resources through *osmosis* – by simply being physically close to Spiritual truth.

In 1 Corinthians 3:2 Paul says, "I fed you with milk and not solid food for you were not yet able to receive it (the solid food)." So, this newborn Christian was fed with *pablum* and not *porterhouse*, because his baby digestive system was not yet able to handle the meat. He was fed with milk. Think back to the definition of milk. Milk is solid food that has been processed through a more mature digestive system. So, Paul, as their Discipler, fed them the more easily digestible truths of doctrine that were given to new Believers. The *solid food* represents the deeper features of orthodoxy and the doctrines of Scripture. The difference is not in kind of truth, but degree of depth. Spiritual immaturity causes one to be unable to receive the depths of truth from the Bible.

Then at the end of verse 2 Paul turns a corner and begins rebuke and correction of these Believers. He said, "…for you are not yet able, for you are still fleshly." Though these Believers had been alive in Christ for some appreciable amount of time, they were still not able to handle the *meat* of Scripture! This would be akin to a 30-year-old sucking on a baby bottle!

Paul uses a different Greek word for *fleshly* in verse 3 than the one he used in verse 1. In verse 3 he uses the word *SarkiNos, not SarkiKos*. The word in verse 3 means to be *willfully, stubbornly, rebelliously fleshly because you refuse to grow up!* This is God's biggest problem, and it is sin! Ouch!

I'm sure some want to argue against this type of Spiritual Immaturity being *sin*, so let's use the hermeneutical principle called the *analogy of scripture* to let the Bible interpret itself. Turn to Hebrews 5:11-14. Here the Bible says, "Concerning him we have much to say and it is hard to explain, since you have become dull of hearing. For through by this time, you ought to be teachers, you have need again for someone to teach you the elementary principles of the oracles of God, and you have come to need milk and not solid food. For everyone who partakes only of milk is not accustomed to the word of righteousness, for he is an infant. But solid food is for the mature, who because of practice have their senses trained to discern good and evil."

The *him* about whom the writer has much to say is *Melchizedek,* the eternal *King/Priest of Salem* who was a *type* of Christ. The writer is saying that he'd like to tell these believers much more about Melchizedek, but they had become *dull of hearing.* Now what does that mean? You once heard well, and this is an acquired deficiency. So here are people who are making progress in their Christian life, and due to willfulness, and stubbornness they became lazy. In fact, the word translated "dull" is the same word across the page, if you will look at Hebrews 6 verse 12. It is the Greek word *nothros,* which literally means *sluggish, lazy, stupid, dull, or slothful.*

In Hebrews 5:12, the author said that, "…by this time you ought to be teachers." In other words, these believers have been in-Christ long enough, exposed to Spiritual truth long enough, that by this time they should've grown enough to be able to teach others these truths. However, instead, these people needed to be taught the "elementary principles of the oracles of God." In the original biblical language this is the word for the *ABC's!* So, here is a student that should be doing doctorate-level work, but is still working to understand the *ABC's of Kindergarten! This is sin!*

It is beyond interesting that we never hear anybody confessing the sin of not growing in Christ. One reason we don't is we don't really place this in the category of *sin*. Another reason is that we don't know how to measure the sin. We don't know how to tell how devastating this sin is.

Tests of Maturity, Found in Hebrews 5.

The Writer of Hebrews gives us 3 tests, by which we may measure the sin of spiritual immaturity.

1) Time Saved. How long in time have you been saved? Let me show you how carefully, carefully, carefully we should study the Bible. You can measure how serious the sin is by measuring how long you've been saved. Hebrews 5:12 says, "by this time you ought to be teachers. " Again, the word *time,* used here, is the Greek word *kronos,* from which we get our word *chronology.* It actually means chronological time. So here is the first way you test how mature you ought to be. How long have you been saved? If you've been saved 6 months you ought to be corresponding in spiritual maturity of 6 months of opportunity. If you've been saved 6 years, you ought to look like a 6-year-old spiritually.

I'm certain that you have been in homes where they have pictures of children by their birthdays on the wall? They have pictures of Year 1, Year 2, Year 3, all the way to what they are now. What if God had spiritual photographs of you like that on His office wall? We'd probably see pictures of some fifty-year-old men, with grey beards, sucking on pacifiers! Think how seriously we should address this problem. And pray over it. Most Believers are about as good as they know how to be. To most, it's about being saved and joining the church. Nobody ever takes those people and *disciples* them, though God clearly *commands* all Believers to *Make Disciples* in His Great Commission, found in Matthew 28:16-20.

2) Truth Heard. Here's the 2nd way or 2nd test of spiritual immaturity. How much truth have you heard and at what level did you listen to it? Hebrews 5:11 says, "...you have become dull of hearing." When we go to corporate worship, we should ask God to let us listen with the maximum level of our being. i.e., do not let me listen just because I'm there. Jesus said, "hearing they will not hear." See Matthew 13:14. Also see Isaiah 6:9; Mark 4:12; Luke 8:10; John 12:40; Acts 28:26, 27; Romans 10;16; 11:8.

I'm reminded of the story of two men talking about their relationships. One of them said, "Does your wife ever talk to herself?" The other one said, "Yeah, but she doesn't know it. She thinks I'm listening." By that definition God must do an awful lot of talking to Himself.

Two ladies were talking about their husbands. One asks the other, "Does Tom ever yell at you." The second woman replied, "Yeah, but when he does, my listening doesn't match his speaking." God blesses us by His very speech in the expectation that we are listening. So very often our listening doesn't match His speaking! We should always be humble to see if our listening matches God's speaking. So, how much truth have you heard and at what level did you listen to it? OK here's number three:

3) Measuring Maturity. How mature should you be and how much impact should you be having in light of how long you've been saved and how much truth you've been exposed to? Look at the little phrase "you ought to be" in Hebrews 5:12. Now here's the way you measure. You measure what you are against what you ought to be in the time you've been saved, how much truth you've been exposed to, and at what level you listened to that truth.

Chapter 5 Hermeneutical Principles
The Law of First Mention

You've, no doubt, heard the old saying, "Practice makes perfect". The only thing wrong with that clique' is that it is wrong! My High School Basketball Coach, Billy B. Smith, was a godly, ultra-conservative, highly skilled educator whose influence left an indelible mark on my life and character. He corrected my view of that old clique' nearly 50 years ago. He said, "Practice only makes perfect if you're practicing a perfect standard. Otherwise, practice doesn't make *perfect,* but rather, practice makes *permanent* that imperfect standard! *Perfect practice makes perfect!"* So, it is critical that we practice the proper standards in our obedience to the command to study God's word in order to show ourselves approved unto Him. We will focus on giving treatment to one of those perfect standards, based on Genesis 3:15, – The Law of First Mention.

There are several generally accepted "rules" of biblical interpretation, or Hermeneutics. One of the critical ones is the *"Law* (or principle or rule) of *First Mention.* The *Law of First Mention* says that, to understand a particular word, concept, or doctrine, the first mention or occurrence of same establishes an unchangeable foundational pattern. The meaning of that word, concept, or doctrine, in context, remains unchanged in the mind of God throughout the Bible. As the Holy Spirit continues to unfold and reveal the mind of God, progressively, throughout the scriptures, He may expand, or give more clarity and information. However, He, the Holy Spirit, never deviates from the original foundational pattern.

> **For example, ignoring the hermeneutical principle of *context* is pervasive in the Body of Christ.**

The book of Genesis is the seed plot for every major doctrine found in the Bible, as every doctrine is found there in its simplest form. God never changes His mind. Immutability is one of His attributes.

Malachi 3:6 says, "For I, the LORD, do not change; therefore, you, O sons of Jacob, are not consumed." James 1:16-17 says, "Do not be deceived, my beloved brethren, every good thing given and every perfect gift is from above, coming down from the Father of lights, with whom there is no variation or shifting shadow."

Psalm 119:89 says, "Forever, O LORD, your word is settled in heaven." The Bible's first mention of a word, concept, or doctrine is the simplest and clearest presentation; Propositions are then more fully developed on that *foundation*. The simple always precedes the complex. So, to fully understand the text of God's revelation, Bible students are advised to process through the grid of sound hermeneutical principles. Prominent among the hermeneutical principles are various matters of Context, including Linguistic, Geographical, Historical, Cultural, Literary context of the passage, book, and entire Bible. When we neglect or ignore application of these principles extreme violence to the word of God results, and we come away with error instead of truth.

For example, ignoring the hermeneutical principle of *context* is pervasive in the Body of Christ. Want proof? One of the dominant gospel presentations employed by Christians is, "God loves you, and He has a plan for your life." Just tune into Christian programming on TV or radio and you're sure to hear this presentation of the gospel repeatedly. If you ask the presenter on what Bible verse or passage this presentation is based, you usually will get a blank stare. If you do get a scripture reference it is likely to be Jeremiah 29:11, which says, "For I know the plans that I have for you, declares the LORD, plans for welfare and not for calamity to give you a future and a hope." In context, this verse has absolutely *nothing* to do with the gospel! It deals with the assurance of God's intentions to bring about blessing in Israel's future.

Let's see another very common example of *context* being ignored or violated. Surely, you've heard some Christian ignore the context of

Matthew 18:20, which says, "For where two or three have gathered together in My name, I am in their midst." The context of this verse includes Matthew 18:15-19, which gives the prescription for church discipline (taboo in the contemporary church). This passage has absolutely *nothing* to do with the idea that where more than one Christian is assembled the Lord promises to be in their midst! This passage, in context, provides the prescription for church discipline! Further, since each Christian carries the Holy Spirit of God inside, Jesus is *always* there with him!

In the context of providing moral directions to the Christians, Hebrews 13:5-6 says, "Make sure that your character is free from the love of money, being content with what you have; for He Himself has said, I will never desert you, nor will I ever forsake you, so that we confidently say, The LORD is my helper, I will not be afraid. What will man do to me?" This is one of the promises of God's ever-abiding presence with the Christian!

These are just two examples of the errors that spring from interpreting scripture devoid of application of each of these critical hermeneutical principles.

Analogy of Scripture

The Analogy of Scripture is also a key hermeneutical principle. This is the practice of allowing scripture to interpret scripture. For example, in describing the work of the word of God in effecting the ongoing process of sanctification in the Christian's life, 2 Corinthians 3:18 says, "But we all, with unveiled face, beholding as in a mirror the glory of the Lord, are being transformed into the same image from glory to glory, just as from the Lord the Spirit." Since Paul doesn't here define the *mirror* for us, we must use the analogy of scripture to help us grasp the proper meaning. So, we search the scripture, in context, for another passage that deals with this concept of doctrine. When we do so, we find that James 1:22-25 is a contextual match. This passage says, "But prove yourselves doers of the word, and not merely hearers who delude themselves. For if anyone is a hearer of the word and not a doer, he is like a man who looks at his natural face in a mirror; for once he has looked at himself and gone away, he has immediately forgotten what kind of person he was. But one who looks intently at the perfect law, the law of liberty, and abides by it, not having become a forgetful hearer but an effectual doer, this man will be blessed in what he does."

In both the Old Testament and the New Testament, God's revealed, inerrant, sufficient, and comprehensive word is called "law". So, in context, James defines the *mirror* as the *perfect law of liberty,* which is the Bible. Accordingly, in 2 Corinthians 3:18 Paul is telling us that the word of God is essential in effecting the sanctification process, as it, the Bible, is what the Holy Spirit uses to transform the Christian. To paraphrase, what the Apostle Paul wrote, "The child of God looks into the word of God looking for the Son of God. Then, the Spirit of God takes the word of God and transforms the child of God, from one stage of glory, to the next, to the next, (the stages are well-nigh infinite) into the very image of the One the child of God is beholding in the mirror (the Bible), which is the Son of God." Consistent and proper application of the aforementioned list of hermeneutical principles is vital if we are to arrive at the truth of what God says in His word.

Conclusion

The Law of First Mention is prominent among all of these principles. A word of caution is in order at this point. It is important to note that no one of these hermeneutical principles is to be ignored, or excluded, in favor of another. Just as God will not sacrifice any one of His attributes to highlight another, so we must not sacrifice any one of these hermeneutical principles to favor another. We'll expose a few key examples in our study.

Chapter 6 The Seed of the woman

First Overt Mention of the Gospel

> **God is supremely jealous of His *Family Portrait Album!***

It is a fact that near Eastern people, especially Hebrews, think in pictures. It is therefore no surprise that the Bible, featuring only one Gentile writer (Luke), is loaded with God's *pictures* describing and illustrating His truth. My Discipler, Herb Hodges, used to routinely, profoundly describe the Bible as *God's Family Portrait Album.* He'd say, "The Old Testament is the portrait *background,* full of shades and shadows that are like fingers pointing to the central figure of the portrait. The *central figure*, sitting for the *portrait,* gloriously displayed in the gospels, is Jesus the Messiah. Then, the epistles are the *garments of glory* that He wears!" God is supremely jealous of His *Family Portrait Album!*

I could only wish that we could allow Moses to give personal testimony about the consequences of marring the *portrait* when he, in a fleshly rage, struck the rock a second time in direct opposition to God's command instructing him to "speak to the rock". In Exodus 17 the Children of Israel were complaining about not having a source of water in their travels through the desert. Beginning in verse 5 God gave Moses' instructions for a remedy. These instructions, in the form of a command, paint a picture of the crucifixion of our Savior, Jesus Christ. In verse 5 God commanded Moses, "Pass before the people and take with you some of the elders of Israel; and take in your hand your staff with which you struck the Nile, and go." So, the *staff* (or rod) was here identified as a staff of *judgement and wrath!* That is identified for us in Exodus 7:17! It is *that staff* - the staff of judgement and wrath, that Moses is to take. God is not finished! In Exodus 17:6, God said, "Behold, I will stand before you there on the rock at Horeb; and you shall strike the rock, and water will come out of it, that the people may drink. And Moses did so in the sight of the elders of Israel." Carefully notice that God said, "I will stand before you there on the rock..." Therefore, in order for Moses to obey the command to *strike the rock* the rod would necessarily strike God!

The command to *strike the rock* represents, in a picture, Jesus, the *rock of our salvation* (Psalm 95:1), taking the judgement and wrath of God upon Himself in paying for our sins! The resulting water pouring forth (as a *type)* represents a picture of the Holy Spirit, who came as a result of Jesus' crucifixion on the cross and His ascension back to the Father (John 16:7)! Hebrews 9:28 tells us, "So Christ also having been offered once to bear the sins of many, will appear a second time for salvation without reference to sin, to those who eagerly await Him." This picture, of Moses striking the rock, illustrates the gospel of Jesus Christ!

Second Overt Mention of the Gospel

The second time the Bible records that the Children of Israel were complaining about not having water is found in Numbers 20. In verse 8-12 we read, "Take the rod (notice it is not here identified as a rod of judgement and wrath as it was in Exodus 7:17); and you and your brother Aaron assemble the congregation and *speak to the rock* before their eyes, that it may yield its water. You shall thus bring forth water for them out of the rock and let the congregation and their beast's drink. So, Moses took the rod from before the LORD, just as He had commanded him; and Moses and Aaron gathered the assembly before the rock. And he said to them, listen now, you rebels; shall we bring forth water for you out of this rock? Then Moses lifted up his hand and *struck the rock twice with his rod:* and water came forth abundantly, and the congregation and their beasts drank. But the LORD said to Moses and Aaron, because you have not believed Me, to treat Me as holy in the sight of the sons of Israel, therefore you shall not bring this assembly into the land which I have given them" (emphasis mine).

The *rock* is a *type* of Jesus, who is the *rock of our salvation.* The striking of the rock represents (in typology) the passion of Jesus being *struck (as it were)* on the cross for our redemption. So, when Moses *struck the rock* a second time, instead of *speaking to the rock,* as God had commanded him to, he (Moses) marred God's Family Portrait Album! As a result, Moses was not permitted to finish his assignment of *leading the sons of Israel into the Promised Land! Speaking to the rock* is what we are to do by praying to the Lord in this post-ascension age! These are pictures pointing to God's plan and His truth. The highest *pursuit* in this life is to find the will of God. The highest *passion* in this life is to perform the will of God. The highest *privilege* in this life is to finish the will of God. Because Moses, in disobedience, marred God's family portrait album, he was denied that highest privilege of finishing the will of God!

Now, immediately someone will say that "the *promise land,* in a picture, represents heaven. So, Jim you're suggesting that Moses didn't go to heaven." I'm suggesting nothing of the sort! The text says that Moses didn't get to lead the Israelites into the promise land. We know Moses, himself, went to heaven. How? In Matthew 17:1-3 we have part of the account of Jesus' *transfiguration.* There we read, "Six days later Jesus took with Him Peter and James and John his brother, and led them up on a high mountain by themselves. And He was transfigured before them; and His face shone like the sun, and His garments became as white as light. And behold, Moses and Elijah appeared to them, talking with Him." 2 Kings 2:11 tells us that Elijah didn't die, but "Elijah went up by a whirlwind into heaven." Since Moses was with Christ and Elijah on the mount of transfiguration, Moses also went to heaven when he died! Even the transfiguration scene is one of God's *pictures!* Moses, the giver of the Law, represents the *Law of God*. Elijah represents *the prophets*. The Law is God's principles and precepts concerning *conduct*. The prophets represent predictions concerning *Christ!* Together, the Law and the Prophets represent what we call the Old Testament, but is better referred to as the *Tanakh*. God's *pictures* abound in His book!

God's *pictures* are immeasurably important to Him. Even the Hebrew alphabet, being highly *pictographic,* conveys the heart of God in the very meaning of the letters. That's a *bridge too far* for purpose of this book, so we'll restrict our study to those biblical pictures that are more easily and readily "unearthed". Unfortunately, we Gentile Christians think in terms of abstract information, and often are totally oblivious to the pictures God wants us to see.

Deity's thesis statement

At this point, we want to explore God's picture of the first overt mention of the gospel given to man, in scripture, in Genesis 3:15; This *picture* points to and illustrates God's plan of redemption – His plan for reconciling man to Himself. If God were writing an essay (such as the Bible), Genesis 3:15 would be considered His "Thesis Statement". The Random House, Inc. Dictionary defines a *thesis statement* this way: "In academic writing, a *thesis statement* is generally a sentence or two that summarizes the main point that an essay, research paper, or speech is making. It is typically located at the end of the introductory paragraph(s). *Thesis Statements* are kind of like roadmaps, laying out for the reader/listener where the writer/speaker is headed (argument) and how they are going to get there (evidence). The *thesis statement* is widely taught in the humanities, especially in English classes in high school and college. It is used to teach students how to make persuasive arguments that cite and analyze evidence and examples researched from literary, historical, and/or other texts." 6

God's *thesis statement,* Genesis 3:15, in a magnificent economy of words, identifies His predetermined remedy for man's fall into sin. Here, immediately after the *fall,* at the beginning of redemptive history, God said to the serpent, "…and I will put enmity between you and the woman, and between your seed and her seed; He shall crush your head and you shall bruise him on the heel." This statement is referred to, in theological terms, as the *Protevangelium.* This is a compound Latin word. The Latin *Protos* means *First. Evangelium* means *Good News,* or *Gospel.* Thus, the *Proto-Evangelium* is commonly referred to as the *First Mention* of the *Gospel* in all of scripture. What we can learn about our God, ourselves, our total depravity, sin, and the Messiah, from God's *thesis statement* encompasses the entire sweep of redemptive history as recorded in scripture. Someone aptly said, "History is *His-Story* – the story of the Messiah, our Lord Jesus Christ.

What are some of the profound truths we can learn from God's "Thesis Statement"? In order to understand, we must first identify the participants involved. So, let's dissect God's *thesis statement* in Genesis 3:15.

Chapter 7 God, Satan, Eve and Adam

The Primary Character, God

God said, "I will..." So, first, we see that the Potentate of the Universe is the power orchestrating this redemptive remedy for man's fall into sin. Whenever man considers the question of *God*, he always considers the proposition relative to God the Father. For example, in man's consideration of the *god* of different religions, and he compares the God of Christianity with the respective *gods* of Islam, Hinduism, Buddhism, etc., he always compares these false deities to God the Father. Man will invariably compare the chief *prophet* of the respective false religions to Jesus. Keep this in mind as we consider this portion of the discourse.

The Bible never stops to try and prove the existence of God. Instead, the Bible assumes His existence! Genesis 1:1 simply says, "In the beginning, God created the heavens and the earth." What beginning you ask? Pick one! Starting at whatever beginning you choose, God already was! Moses gives us this proposition in Psalm 90. In verse 2 he writes, "Before the mountains were brought forth, or ever Thou had formed the earth and the world, from everlasting to everlasting, Thou art God." In this tremendous doctrinal statement about God, Moses tells us that God is the only God... "Thou art God." He tells us that God is infinite and eternal... "From everlasting to everlasting." He also tells us that God is the creator-the source of all that is... "Before the mountains were made, before you formed the earth and the world..." In this great Psalm it is obvious that Moses is expressing, or describing, the character of God in contrast to the finiteness, powerlessness, sinfulness, and dependent state of man.

In Psalm 90:10 he writes, "Man lives seventy years; and if he's really strong he lives eighty years. But even after those eighty years, he finds that his strength, his labor and sorrow, it is soon cut off, and we fly away." In Psalm 90:1 Moses writes, "Lord, Thou hast been our dwelling place in all generations. We've always found our refuge in You. We've always had to face our own inadequacies and our frailties, and we've always known that the only strength was Your strength." So, again, God is eternal, the all-powerful creator, and the strength of His people. Simple minded, heathen man has always proposed that Christians have simply invented this God as a sort of *crutch* to prop himself up in dealing with life. So, the question, relative to the existence of God, becomes, *is He?*

Satan

Next, we know that Satan, who is using the Serpent, is the one God is addressing in Genesis 3:15. It is his head that will be *crushed.* How do we know that? Satan is not here mentioned by name. In Hebrew the word is *Nacash.* It is the name for a reptilian type of animal – more of a dragon type creature. Most people assume it is a snake. You always see little pictures of the snake wound around a tree or slithering up, but the Bible doesn't support that. The word for *serpent,* used here, means "to hiss". In Genesis 3:14, part of the curse was that he would go on his belly. So, in some measure this appears as an upright animal.

There's another Old Testament word used to speak of reptiles. It is *Tanine.* It is used interchangeably with *Nacash.* There's a section of Exodus 7:9-15 where Moses is having a showdown with magicians in Pharaoh's court. These magicians throw down their sticks and their sticks become *Tanine.* This was evil manifesting great "works", and it can still happen today! (See Matthew 7:22-23, "Lord, Lord, did we not prophesy in Your name, and in Your name cast out demons, and in Your name perform many miracles?") But when Moses throws down his staff it becomes a serpent called *Nacash.* So, from that text we can conclude that they're used interchangeably, although *Tanine* is the word that appears for *dragon or sea monster. Nacash,* then is some kind of reptile like

Tanine. It could be a snake after the curse and/or after the flood. We don't know what form reptiles took. We don't know what reptiles got on the ark and therefore got off, and what other ones were destroyed. It was some kind of reptile – some kind of dragon.

There's something different about this particular reptile because he said to the woman, *"Indeed has God said you shall not eat from any tree of the garden?"* This particular reptile speaks. We have no biblical record of any of the other animals in the Garden speaking. This particular reptile knows about God. This particular reptile has a personality. This particular reptile speaks with intelligence. This particular reptile has a devious, malevolent, evil mind. This is not a fable, as some have suggested. Nothing in here tells you "Let me make up a story to illustrate how sin came." It doesn't say that. This is not a legend with a moral, as others have suggested. There is no moral. If this is a fable, then how do you curse a fable in verse 14? The text says that God cursed the serpent! This is not a legend, fable, nor parable with a moral. This is the word of God!

This is a crafty, subtle, malevolent, evil, wicked individual reptile, because it is being used by a super human intelligence to lead the Woman and Adam into a choice for evil. This personality had already made that choice. This personality inside that animal knew the effect of the choice Adam and the Woman were being tempted to make. This is a reptile that hates God. This is a reptile that is angry about the circumstance in which he has found himself.

Why is this personality, using this reptile, angry? He had already made a choice to overthrow God and take over God's throne. Not only did he fail, but his attempted coup resulted in him being demoted and kicked out of heaven. He still has some access to God, and we know that because of his dialogue with God over tempting Job.

Hear the very words of God from Isaiah 14:12-15. "How you have fallen from heaven, O star of the morning, Son of the dawn! You have been cut down to the earth, you who have weakened the nations! But you said in your heart, *I will* ascend to the heaven; *I will* raise my throne above the stars of God, and *I will* sit on the mount of assembly in the recesses of the north. *I will* ascend above the heights of the clouds; *I will* make myself like the "Most High." Nevertheless, you will be thrust down to Sheol, to the recesses of the pit" (emphasis mine). Now, I know someone will say, "Well, that was written about the King of Babylon." In Luke 10:18 and Revelation 12:8-10, God refers to Isaiah 14:12-15 (quoted above) to describe Satan's fall! This is far more than a reference to the human King of Babylon, who could not fall from heaven because he'd never been there! Just as the LORD addressed Satan in His words to the serpent in Genesis 3:14-15, this word of the Lord speaks to the King of Babylon and to the devil who energized him.

Let's see another passage attesting to this fact. In Ezekiel 28:12-17 God said, "Son of man, take up a lamentation over the King of Tyre and say to him, Thus, says the Lord God, You, had the seal of perfection, Full of wisdom and perfect in beauty. You were in Eden, the garden of God; Every precious stone was your covering; The ruby, the topaz, and the diamond; The beryl, the onyx, and the jasper; The lapis lazuli, the turquoise and the emerald; and the gold, the workmanship of your settings and sockets was in you. On the day that you were created they were prepared. You were the anointed cherub who covers and I placed you there. You were on the holy mountain of God; You walked in the midst of the stones of fire. You were blameless in your ways from the day you were created until unrighteousness was found in you. By the abundance of your trade, you were internally filled with violence. And you sinned; Therefore, I have cast you as profane from the mountain of God and I have destroyed you. O covering cherub, from the midst of the stones of fire. Your heart was lifted up because of your beauty; You corrupted your wisdom by reason of your splendor. I cast you to the ground."

There are, obviously, things in this passage that could not possibly apply to a human king! This describes the "Anointed Cherub", which refers to Satan (Lucifer) in his exalted privilege as an angel guarding (covering) God's throne, as cherubim guarded Eden (Gen 3:24). Satan (Lucifer) originally had continuous and unrestricted access to the glorious presence of God! This is the personality who is using this reptile in Genesis 3. This is the personality upon whom God levied the curse. His own expulsion from the throne room of God is why he is so evil and malevolent, and has such hatred toward the God of the universe!

This evil, wicked personality, using the reptile, wants to pull the wonderful new creation down. He must have looked at the creation of Adam and Eve and thought, "this isn't anything like I've known. Angels don't procreate. What is this *"multiply and replenish the earth, and fill the earth"* stuff? They've been given sovereignty over these wondrous creatures. This isn't anything like I've known." The fact that he was cursed is proof that he was a responsible moral being. 9

Who was using this creature? Go to the back of the Bible to Revelation. We must take the whole council of God here, because you really don't get the clear identification of him in Genesis 3. Nothing in Genesis 3 is said about Satan. Neither is Sin mentioned in Genesis 3, though it is clear, beginning in Genesis 4, that's where it began in mankind. So, we go to the end of the Bible to find out who he is from the book of Revelation 12:9. Here we find these two terms that are basically borrowed from the Hebrew where the reptile is called *Nacash* and *Tanine*, which is both serpent and dragon. Verse 9 says, *"And the great dragon was thrown down, the serpent of old who is called the devil and Satan..."* Now there is a very clear designation. Who was using this reptile in the Garden? Who was using that dragon? Who is that original one of old who deceives the whole world? It is none other than the devil and Satan! There he is clearly identified.

The attitude of Satan is captured in a famous poem in these words, "All is not lost, the unconquerable will, and study of revenge, immortal hate, and the courage never to submit or yield." (*Paradise Lost* by John Milton). It was pride that resulted in his sin and resulted in Lucifer being kicked out of heaven. Satan is delighted when men think of him as a character in a red suit with horns and a pitchfork! That hides the reality of what a wicked, vile, powerful, malevolent being! Don't be duped by the vision of the cartoon character! The enemy of men's souls is very much real and dangerous!

CS Lewis ably depicts Satan's cunning and craftiness in tempting humans in his classic allegorical book, *The Screwtape Letters*. I highly recommend this to my readers. This is the best description, outside the Bible, of the way the enemy of men's souls works. As one of the events in this book is told, the senior demon, Screwtape, is reviewing the ineffective temptation tactics of his junior demon Nephew, Wormwood, who is trying to tempt this old holy hermit to sin. This hermit had left society, many years before, to live alone in the wilderness and contemplate holiness. After watching Wormwood's tactics, Screwtape pulled him aside and said, "What you are doing is much too crude. Please, permit me." Then Screwtape leaned into the hermit's ear and whispered quietly, *"Your brother was just named the Bishop of Alexandria."* Immediately, a deep scowl, green with envy, flushed over the old hermit's face as he clenched his fists and teeth! Upon seeing this, Screwtape turned to Wormwood, with a smile, and said, "You see...this is precisely the sort of thing I recommend." What a vivid picture of the cunning, craftiness, and malevolence of Satan! It was he who used the serpent to tempt Eve to sin in the Garden of Eden. Satan is the father of lies.

John 8:44 says, "You are of your father the devil, and the lusts of your father you will do. He was a murderer from the beginning, and abode not in the truth, because there is no truth in him. When he speaks a lie, he speaks of his own: for he is a liar, and the father of lies." It was Satan, using this dragon-like creature, who tempted Eve to sin and led to the fall of all mankind. What is sin? Any want of conformity to the law of God. Sin came to the human race, not through Eve, but through Adam, who followed the words of his wife instead of the word of God! Romans 5:12 says, "Therefore, just as through one-man sin entered the world, and death through sin, and thus death spread to all men, because all sinned..." This malevolent fallen angel, Satan, is yet the enemy of mankind. His strategy, deployed against Adam and Eve in the Garden of Eden, has not changed. There he sought to *disarm* them of the word of God. This, his perennial strategy, is still being deployed against the people of God right now! Beware!

Eve

When God finished creating the animals, He brought each before Adam to see what he would name them. Man, what a slap in the face of Evolution! Do you know anyone who can name every type of animal that God created? No, me neither! So, we've not evolved, but *devolved!* By doing this, among other things, God was showing Adam that He had given Adam dominion over these creatures. Also, He wanted Adam to see that none of these creatures had the same body, features, and faculties that he had. In other words, none were suitable to be a match for Adam. God had pronounced all of His creation to be "good". However, when He saw that Adam had no mate to correspond to him, God said, "not good" (Genesis 2:18). God said that for Adam there was no "suitable helper" (vs 20). In

Genesis 2:21, we see how God made the woman to be Adam's "suitable helper". "So, the LORD God caused a deep sleep to fall upon the man, and he slept; then He took one of his ribs and closed up the flesh at that place (the first surgery & the first act of divine healing). The LORD God fashioned into a woman the rib which He had taken from the man, and brought her to the man. The man said, 'This is now bone of my bones, and flesh of my flesh; She shall be called Woman, because she was taken out of man. For this reason, a man shall leave his father and his mother, and be joined to his wife; and they shall become one flesh. And the man and his wife were both naked and were not ashamed.'"

Notice, God could've taken a sample from any part of Adam's body, but He took a rib from his side. No, this does not support the myth that men have one less rib than women! There are people born that way (both men and women), but that is an anomaly that is a physical problem. The vast majority of people are born with 12 sets of ribs, no matter their gender.

When you combine the location of the sample with the fact that God said she was to be Adam's "suitable helper", and the fact that God brought her to see what Adam would name her, we can draw several conclusions. First, Adam is given the role of "head" of the new family. She is to be his "helper". Next, God took the sample from Adam's side. He did not take it from Adam's head, so the woman is not to lead Adam! (When Adam followed his wife, instead of leading her, the human race fell!) God didn't take the sample from Adam's foot, so Adam was not to walk on her! He took the sample from Adam's *side,* so she was to come alongside, submit to his headship, and help him. Finally, Adam called her *woman* (Hebrew – Isha) because she came from *man* (Hebrew – Ish). This is the biblical reason that when a man marries a woman, she takes his name.

News Flash...God is NOT politically correct!

Now, I know that this biblical account of how God created the first family is not politically correct in modern times. News Flash...God is NOT politically correct! It was God's plan that through this nuclear family structure, the man and woman made in His image, would multiply and fill the earth with others made in His image. Genesis chapter 2 is an expansive narrative of the creation that happened in Genesis chapter 1. In other words, Genesis 2 does not represent a *different* creation account. It is simply an expanded explanation of the creation account given in Genesis 1. In Genesis 1:27-28 we read, "God created man in His own image, in the image of God He created him; male and female (no third possibility) He created them. God blessed them; and God said to them, Be fruitful and multiply, and fill the earth and subdue it; and rule over the fish of the sea and over the birds of the sky and over every living thing that moves on the earth."

God gave Genesis 2:24 for Adam and the woman's (she was not yet named Eve) progeny; That would be us. How do we know that? Because neither Adam nor the woman, had a human father or mother!

Then God tells us, in verse 25, "And the man and his wife were both naked and were not ashamed." Remember, this was before their fall into sin through disobedience. Therefore, with no knowledge of evil, even their nakedness was innocent and without shame. They were completely satisfied and gratified in their one union and in their relationship and service to God. They were made in perfection, so they had no sinful inward principle to tempt them. Thus, the solicitation to sin had to come from the outside. Satan, working through the serpent, was all too ready to provide that opportunity!

Adam

The one final participant we need to identify, as we dissect God's Thesis Statement (Genesis 3:15) is Adam. He's the most important person in this story that is not God. Why? For several reasons. Romans 6:23 tells us that, "...the wages of sin is death, but the free gift of God is eternal life in Christ Jesus our Lord." Romans 5:12-14 says, "Therefore, just as through one-man sin entered into the world, and death through sin, and so death spread to all men, because all sinned, for until the Law sin was in the world, but sin is not imputed where there is no law. Nevertheless, death reigned from Adam until Moses, even over those who had not sinned in the likeness of the offense of Adam, who is a type of Him who was to come." God is telling us, here, exactly where sin originated in mankind. All men from Adam to Moses were subject to death, not because of their sinful acts against the Mosaic law (which they did not have yet), but because of their own sinful nature inherited from Adam! Adam was the *representative head of the human race.* Therefore, every person, born as a result of the union between two mere humans, is born with a sinful nature inherited from Adam. 1 Corinthians 15:21-22 says, "For since by a man came death, by a man also came the resurrection of the dead. As in Adam all die. So, in Christ all are made alive."

God only (this in no way diminishes God's act of creation. He's the only one Who can create!) *created* every other creature, including angels. However, God acted specially and *generated* life in the nostrils of man. Genesis 2:7 says, "Then the LORD God formed man of dust from the ground, and breathed into his nostrils the breath of life; and man became a living being." So, *life* in Adam was *generated.* By extension, because the woman was taken from Adam, the same is true of Eve. This is why human beings are *generated. Therefore, they have the possibility of being regenerated* through faith in Jesus Christ (the seed of the woman). *Regeneration* is not possible for God's only other *moral* creatures, which are angels. They are simply *created* and not made in God's image, nor was life *generated* in them. Accordingly, they cannot be *regenerated.* So those who are fallen (Satan and the third of the angels that he convinced to follow him – see Rev 12) are incorrigible and cannot be redeemed!

I remember, when she was about 8 years old, my daughter, Jayme, asked, "Daddy, since Satan is the one causing the problem, why don't God just save him?" I told her that I'd answer her question later, and proceeded to spend the next several hours reducing the explanation (above) to the level of understanding of my 8-year-old! Think that's not a herculean task? You try it sometime! I later explained to Jayme that since God is one, displaying Himself in 3 persons, Father, Son, and Holy Spirit, He made us in His image. Man is also *triune* as he consists of *spirit, soul,* (mind emotions and will)*, and body* (1 Thessalonians 5:23). This is why we have the ability to be related to God through faith in Jesus Christ. Satan, who is an angel that sinned against God, was not made in God's image and, therefore, cannot be saved.

The point is, by being created in the image of God, and having God *generate* life in him, man is God's highest creation signature! Since the *seed* of human life originates in Adam, he became the *federal head,* or *representative head,* of the entire human race. Every *mere* human born in this world, after Adam, carries Adam's *seed.* That seed was passed through Seth, and his descendants, down to Noah and his sons. So, there's only *one Race,* and that is the *Human Race!* There are many ethnicities, but only one *Race!* Remember, *Truth is what God says!*

Listen to this from Webster's 1828 dictionary. Webster defines *race* as this, "The lineage of a family or continued series of descendants from a parent who is called a stock. A *race* is the series of descendants indefinitely, thus by definition, all mankind is called the *race* of Adam."

Listen to Paul in Acts 17:26. "And he made from one (some Greek manuscripts read *one blood*) man every nation of mankind to live on all the face of the earth, having determined allotted periods and the boundaries of their dwelling place." Paul is hearkening back to Genesis chapter 10:32. God made from one man every nation of men. There are not multiple *races* of men. There is but *one race* of man. What we have in Genesis chapter 10 is not the table of *races*, but the table of *nations*. That is what we have in Genesis 10, single parentage, single lineages, *not races*.

A geneticist, a computer scientist, and a geologist, at Yale decided to corroborate on research based on what we know of genealogy. They discovered that you could go back in time only 2000 to 5000 years to find somebody who could count every person alive today as a descendant! By the way, these are not Christians. These are evolutionary Scientists. Well, interesting enough, the flood happened about 4000 years ago. Wow!

Now, according to the Bible, the earth is only about 6000 years old. If you read the research produced by the *Institute of Creation Research* (a group of Paleontologists, and other Scientists), they provide peer-reviewed, scientific evidence that points to the earth being only around 6000 years old, not billions and billions of years old. The aforementioned Evolutionary Scientists say, furthermore, if you go back 5000 to 7000 years everybody living today has exactly the same set of ancestors! That would be Adam and Eve. One race! Our culture says there are multiple races. The Bible says that there is but one! If the Church would stand on this truth that clearly says we're all the same, and begin from that point of commonality, substantial progress could be made in *Ethnic Relations!*

Since God says that all humans come from Adam's *seed,* this makes all human beings of the *race* of Adam. He is, therefore, the *federal head, or representative head* of the entire human race. So, when Adam sinned, because we were in his loins, we sinned. When Adam came under the condemnation of God, we came under the condemnation of God. His history (after the fall) is our history! However, in order to get a *panoramic view* of how God advanced His promise of providing "the seed of the woman" (Genesis 3:15) we must begin in Genesis 5 and paint the picture through *"The Sons of Promise".*

Chapter 8 Beyond Sigmund Freud to Truth

Freud's Foundations

Sigmund Freud (considered by academia to be one of history's greatest Philosophers) said that man *created* God – the exact opposite of what the Bible says, that God created man. The Viennese Psychiatrist's book *The Future of an Illusion* is still required reading in many Humanities courses at major universities around the world. In this book Freud postulates that man so desperately needs security. He said that because man has such deep-seated fear, and because he lives in a threatening world in which he has very little control over his circumstances, he invented a *god* to get him out when he needed something. Freud said that "God was invented by man for three reasons."

- Number one: *Man fears the unpredictability, the impersonality, and the ruthlessness of nature*. In other words, he sees disease, famine, and disasters and knows that he doesn't have any defense against any of these things, and he *imagines* somebody who can deliver him.

- Secondly, Freud said man was caused to invent God because *man is afraid because of his relationships to his fellow man*. Because man so often feels that he always gets a raw deal from his fellow man he imagines a sort of divine, *cosmic umpire* with a divine whistle who can stop play and give everybody what they deserve.

- Thirdly, Freud said that man has invented God because *he's afraid of death and extinction*. So, he wants to find a heavenly Father, a happy person somewhere, who will take him to a happy place, because he can't stand the fact that he would go out of existence. Freud posited that in doing this man imagines a place called heaven.

Freud said that man conjures up *God* in his mind because man fears the unpredictability of nature, is afraid of relationships with fellow man, and he fears death.

Now, this is Freud's view of God. There is no God except in the figment of man's imaginations. There is no proof for that. That was created in Freud's own corrupted, unregenerate mind, as were all of the other things that Freud came up with. This is even an *ignorant* view of *religion*. When you thoroughly investigate *religion,* you find that when man manufactures a god, he is seldom a god who can deliver. He is usually an oppressive, demanding, despot that must be continually appeased! Where men have invented gods (as they have in all false religions), they are not super-protector gods; They are gods that men fear! Do you suppose the woman in India who takes her baby and throws it to drown in the Ganges River thinks of that god as a great savior, a great *universal umpire*, somebody to deliver her from her problems? Not on your life! She looks at that god as some great, fearful ogre who must be appeased!

Truth Illustration, India

Listen to this real-life story from a friend who is an indigenous Missionary in India. As he walked along the banks of the Ganges, Varghese encountered a woman beating her chest with her fists as she wailed in grief. He knelt beside her and asked her problem. She replied, "The problems in my home are too many, and my sins are heavy on my heart, so I offered the best I have to my goddess (Ganga): my firstborn son." With horror, Varghese realized the woman had just thrown her infant into the Ganges River! He began telling her about Jesus, about how He loved her and her baby, and about how her sins could be forgiven through Him. Through the swimming of her tears she replied, "I have never heard that before! Why couldn't you have come 30 minutes earlier? If you had, my child would not have died." How tragic is this? This woman believed that if she "gave the best she had to her goddess" this deity would be appeased and take away the problems in her home and take away the burden of sin she lived under! This is unassailable proof that (as usual) the Persian Poet (Freud) is wrong in his assessment of why people do what they do! As an aside...

> **I am not amazed by what people will not believe,**
> **but rather, what they will fall for!**

The Ganges is considered a *tirtha* (which means a crossing point) between heaven and earth. At a *tirtha,* prayers and sacrifices are thought most likely to reach the gods and remove sin and, in the other direction, blessings can descend most readily from heaven. The river is, along with two other sites, the location of the extraordinary Kumbha Mela ritual which dates back to at least the 7th century CE. Now held every three years, Hindu pilgrims of all social status perform a ritual bathing in the river which is thought to purify body and soul, wash away karma, and bring good fortune. I have personally witnessed this event, involving from *70 to 100 million people*, which grows ever bigger and can claim to be the largest human gatherings in history. Along the banks of each side of the Ganges there are shaving booths. There, the worshippers have all hair shaved from their bodies and captured. This is because they believe that 10 years of immortality is granted for each individual hair given to the deity through the Ganges. A Shaman leads the procession into the water where worshippers deposit there "hair offerings". Waters from the Ganges are also collected by believers and taken home for use in rituals and as an offering. Drops from the river are also dropped into the mouth before a body is cremated. This is the type of god that man invents. After witnessing this worship ceremony, I came away having been profoundly impacted by this truth; I am not amazed by what people will not believe, but rather, what they will fall for!

God, Real or Invented by Man?

> **Rather than *invent a god*, man would rather that God did not exist at all! Man does his best to eliminate God.**

Rather than *invent a god,* man would rather that God did not exist at all! Man does his best to eliminate God. Why? If God exists that means that man is not ultimately in charge of his own life! That's what 1 John 2:16 calls the "boastful pride of life". That verse says, "For all that is in the world, the lust of the flesh and the lust of the eyes and the boastful pride of life is not from the Father, but is from the world." This, man's sin problem, began in the Garden of Eden, and continues today! Genesis 3:6 says, "When the woman *saw* that the tree was good for food, and that it was a *delight to the eyes,* and that the tree was *desirable to make one wise...*" There it is...the lust of the eyes, the lust of the flesh (good for food), and the pride of life (desirable to make one wise), in other words, *the wise must be in charge!* What happened immediately after man's fall in the garden? Immediately Adam and Eve hid themselves from God. They began to wish that God didn't exist; and that has been the perpetual attitude of sinful man throughout history! That's man's ultimate issue; I want to be in charge of me! Conversely, if/since God exists, that means that I'm not in charge!

Romans 1:19-21 says, "because that which is known about God is evident within them (man) for God made it evident to them. For since the creation of the world His invisible attributes, His eternal power, and divine nature, have been clearly seen being understood through what has been made, so that they are without excuse. For even though they knew God, they did not honor Him as God or give thanks, but they became futile in their speculations, and their foolish heart was darkened." Man has not *made* God; Man has wished God did not exist! God is! As is clear from the Bible, God made man!

The evidence is very clear that God exists. I don't think that you can just strike aside all evidence, and say there is no God, and then invent a theory like man making God, without really ignoring some very startling truth.

Chapter 9 Reasons to Believe in God

Theologians have cataloged the reasons we believe in God in many ways. One such catalog I'll just list for you. Theologians can't *prove* God, but they can certainly show us that there's more reason to believe in God than reason not to believe in Him. Listen to this. As Christians, we accept one big miracle: God, and everything else makes sense. An atheist denies God, and has to have a miracle for every other thing; and they say it takes too much faith to believe in God. Obviously, it takes a *lot more faith* to be an atheist than it does to be a Christian! The following represents only 6 of the plethora of arguments for belief In God.

Teleological Argument

For example, there's what theologians call a *teleological argument*. That comes from the Greek word *teleios*, which means perfection, or result, or end, or finish. We look at something that is perfected, or finished, or done, and we say it's a design, and it must have had a designer. You can take your wall clock apart and put all of the individual pieces in a bag and shake the bag as long and as often as you like, but you'll never hear it tick again! You know that when you have something that works, somebody made it work. Intelligent design implies a designer.

Ontology

A second argument used for God's existence is the argument from *ontology*. *Ontos* is a Greek participle referring to the verb "to be," a being of God. The suffix *ology* means *the study of.* So *Ontology* is the study of the being of God. The very fact that man can conceive of God in the terms that truly intimate God's character indicates He exists. For example, *thirst* posits that somewhere there is something to quench that thirst.

Aesthetics

A third argument for God is from *aesthetics*. People say because there is beauty, and because there is truth, there has to be somewhere in the universe the standard on which beauty and truth are based. Since there's nothing that matches the beauty of God's creation, there must exist a being in whom this quality exists. Since truth is absolute, there must exist a being in whom this attribute is contained.

Volition

Fourthly, there is the *volitional* argument for the existence of God. Every day, man faces a myriad of choices. Man has a *volition* (will) to make those choices. Because there is an ability for a man to express an *individual* will, there must be somewhere an *infinite will* that created this; and the world must be, as it is, the expression of that *infinite* will. We humans are finite. God is infinite. Since the finite being has a will, his Creator must also have an infinite will.

Morality

Fifthly, there is the argument from *morality* for the existence of God. The very fact that we know there is right and wrong demands the necessity of an absolute standard. If there did not exist the concept of right and wrong the universe would destroy itself through chaos. Even men in the most aboriginal situation have an innate sense of right and wrong. In order for this to be as it is, the Creator of man must have morality (the absolutes of right and wrong) as one of His attributes.

Cosmology

Number six is the argument from *cosmology* – not as one person said, cosmetology. *Cosmology*; big difference. *Cosmology* is the argument of *cause and effect*. This is the concept that says *for every effect there exists a cause.* That rule encompasses everything except God Himself. *God* is exclusive. Thus, no *cause exists for the existence of God.* You see, there are only two views of the universe: either God is, and that makes sense; or God is not, and then we've got some problems. The concept of *nothing times nobody equals everything* is ludicrous!

Summary

For example, the equation of "God is not" says *nobody times nothing equals everything.* That's a little difficult to believe. The other possibility is *somebody times something out of nothing equals everything*, and that makes sense. You see, cosmology is the argument from cause and effect: The Greek word *kosmos* means *world*, the effect, the universe. We look at it, and we say somebody made it. As we define the world, we learn more about the One who made it. That's Romans 1:20 – quoted above. For example,

- The cause of *perpetual motion* must be powerful.
- The cause of *complexity* must be omniscient.
- The cause of *consciousness* must be personal.
- The cause of *feeling* must be emotional.
- The cause of *will* must be volitional.
- The cause of *ethical values* must be moral.
- The cause of *religious values* must be spiritual.
- The cause of *beauty* must Himself be aesthetic.
- The cause of *righteousness* must be holy.
- The cause of *justice* must be just.
- The cause of *love* must be loving.
- The cause of *life* must be living.

All you need to do is look at what we have in the world and look at it carefully, and you'll see that there must be a God who is infinite, eternal, omnipotent, omnipresent, omniscient, personal, emotional, volitional, moral, spiritual, aesthetic, holy, just, loving, and living. It's all there. When you study the Bible, it never seeks to prove the existence of the Father. It assumes His existence, and the Bible substantiates every aspect of His nature and character. God is.

Chapter 10 The Trinity

The Bible unequivocally presents God as a *Trinity – Three personages in One God.* Many have attempted to give practical illustrations of this. For example, some have tried to illustrate this divine truth by using a tree. They say the root, trunk, and branches illustrate the Trinity. The illustration cannot be used for the Trinity, as it fails to demonstrate inseparable *unity* while simultaneously illustrating *individual identity.* In other words, the unity is inseparable in that if one is present all 3 are present, and if one is absent the *whole* is non-existent. You see, one can cut a piece of the root of certain trees and plants and that piece will eventually sprout a new tree! In this case all 3 *individually identifiable* parts are not required for existence!

Another illustration of the Trinity that is commonly used is that of *water* in its 3 different states, i.e., …*liquid, solid, and gas.* This is a dismal failure in illustrating the Trinity for a couple of reasons. First, all 3 *individually identifiable* entities cannot be present simultaneously. Second, an outside *agent* or *force* is required to *change* water from one state to the next. This would illustrate the ancient heresy of *Modalism* believing that God acts in three different modes. The one true God functions as Father, then *changes* to function as Son, then *changes* to function as the Holy Spirit! This *Modalistic representation* of the Trinity is heretical! The universe, itself, speaks to the Trinitarian nature of the one true God. Following table contributed by Charlie Liebert. charlie@sixdaycreation.com

The three-fold nature of the Universe

Item/Subject	One	Two	Three
Matter	Proton	Electron	Neutron
Time	Yesterday	Today	Tomorrow
States of matter	Gas	Liquid	Solid

Primary Colors	Yellow	Blue	Red
Universe	Matter	Energy	Motion
Egg	Shell	Yolk	White
Family	Father	Mother	Child
Mankind	Body	Soul	Spirit
God	Father	Son	Holy Spirit
Soul	Mind	Emotions	Will
Emotions	Physiological Response	Cognitive Label	Emotional Response
Secular "Mind"	Thinking	Feeling	Doing
Quiz Questions	Animal	Vegetable	Mineral
Rocks - Geology	Igneous	Metamorphic	Sedimentary
Planet Earth	Crust	Mantle	Core
Photosynthesis	Light	Chlorophyll	Chemistry
Plato's Soul	Reason	Spirit	Appetite
Greek Matter Understanding	Air	Fire	Water
Radiation	Alpha	Beta	Gamma
Water Molecule	Hydrogen	Oxygen	Hydrogen
3-Legged Stool	Most Stable of	All Tables	Even 4 Legs
Ear	Outer	Middle	Inner
Natural Forces	Electromagnetic	Gravitational	Nuclear
Newton Motion Laws	Inertia	Momentum	Action/Reaction
Quadratic Equation	aX^2	bX	c
Thermodynamics	Temperature	Energy	Entropy

The Bible presents *God* as 3 *individually identifiable* personalities in *one* essence. In other words, though the Father is *other* than the Son, and the Son is *other* than the Spirit, and the Spirit is *other* than the Father or the Son, they are of the same *essence*. This relationship is adequately illustrated by the three dimensions of Space.

SPACE

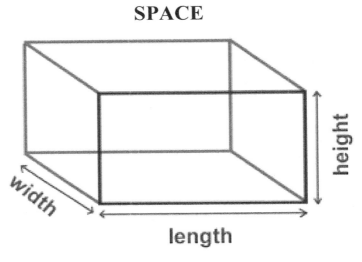

length

In order to have *space* you must have 3 *individually identifiable* dimensions – *Height, Width, and Length.* If any one of these 3 individually identifiable dimensions is missing you do *not* have space, but rather, only an *image.* Though they are *individually identifiable*, they are of the same *essence.* In other words, all of the *space* in a cube consists 100% of *Height, Width, and Length.* So, all of *space* is of the same *essence* though the *dimensions* remain eternally individually identifiable. So, it is with the Trinity of God. Each is *individually identifiable.* However, if any one of these individually identifiable personages is missing, you no longer have *God.* They are co-equal, co-essential, and co-eternal!

Jesus Is of the Same Essence as the Father

Since Jesus is of the same *essence* as the Father, let's see how the Apostle John introduces Him. In his gospel, the Apostle John's purpose statement is given in John 20:31. It says, "...but these have been written so that you may believe that Jesus is the Christ, the Son of God; and that believing you may have life in His name."

Since John seeks to establish the deity of Jesus, John 1:1,2 starts in the same place the Bible begins. Here, John wrote, "In the beginning was the Word, and the Word was with God, and the Word was God. He was in the beginning with God." In the original language of the New Testament, Greek, the word translated *was* literally means *always was*. The word translated *with,* is the Greek word *pros.* It is an association preposition that means *face-to-face.* This means that Jesus always was *co-equal, co-essential, and co-eternal* with God!

John 1:14, continues in development of God's *thesis statement* when it says, "And the Word became flesh, and dwelt among us, and we saw His glory, glory as of the only begotten from the Father, full of grace and truth." Finally, in John 1:17 we read, "For the Law was given through Moses; grace and truth were realized through Jesus Christ." So, as the second member of the Trinity, Jesus, was there before the beginning inside the "Godhood". Oh, and in case you were wondering, the Holy Spirit, the third member of the Trinity, was there at the beginning also.

Genesis 1:2 says, "The earth was formless and void, and darkness was over the surface of the deep, and the Spirit of God was moving over the surface of the waters." The One True God, manifested in 3 persons, always was...before what we know as "the beginning". The Bible begins with God, and then progressively exposes the many facets of His nature and character, and develops His *thesis*. This is crucial if we are to understand as much about God as is humanly possible with finite minds. Author's Note: For further study of the Trinity go to Truth & Life Ministries.org and see the author's study entitled *Doctrine of the Trinity.*

The late Pastor, Bob "Chef" Morey, founder of *Faith Defenders*, said it oh so well, so I'll quote him. He said, "The very first thing that God wants us to understand about Himself is that He is the Creator of heaven and earth. Thus, the very first attribute is that God is the Creator. In the beginning, God created the heavens and the earth (Genesis 1:1). The early Church understood this in a deeply profound way. They faced a pagan world that believed the universe was eternal and whatever gods existed were only finite parts of this world. Thus, according to the early Church, the first essential difference between the Christian God and the gods of the pagans was that He is the "Maker of Heaven and Earth."" [7]

All of the other attributes of God make sense only in the context of a God who existed prior to, independent of, and apart from the space-time universe that He created out of nothing for His own glory. If God is not the Creator, then He is not GOD. If someone accepts this fact, he will have few, if any, problems with accepting anything else in Scripture. Who can give a "coherent" explanation of Creation? Who can know the mind of the Creator and tell us the how's, whys, and wherefores of Creation? We must bow, in humility and awe, before the God who is there in the very first sentence of His revelation. We must confess that creation out of nothing is beyond human reason and experience. This is why the author of Hebrews stated, "Faith is the conviction of things not seen" (Hebrews 11:1). The world focuses its main attack on the Biblical doctrine of creation. In the absence of divine creation, God becomes just one of many gods, all of whom derive their existence from the world!

To, again quote "Chef Bob", "The doctrine of creation is always the starting point throughout Scripture in any discussion of the "Gordian knots" (extremely difficult or involved problems) of theology. Thus, when Paul dealt with the issue of Divine sovereignty and man's moral accountability in Romans 9, he immediately turned the discussion to the doctrine of creation (vv. 20-21). When dealing with why wives are to submit to their husbands, he appealed to creation (1 Corinthians 11:7-9; 1 Timothy 2:12-13)."

The Bible *assumes* the existence of the one true God. I'll illustrate. Suppose that you had zero mechanical ability. The only thing you knew about a car was where to add the gas. Then, suppose I brought you a truck load of auto parts, with no markings, and no illustrated photos or schematics, and asked you to examine these parts and identify the vehicle by make and model; Then assemble the parts to make that vehicle. Performing such tasks would likely be totally hopeless for the vast portion of humanity. However, let's suppose that I brought you the fully assembled vehicle, and a manual, with pictures, fully delineating each individual fastener and part. Then, suppose that I asked you to identify the vehicle and disassemble it. The outcome between the two scenarios would reveal a huge difference in the degree of success! Now, this is exactly the way the Bible *assumes* the existence of God, and then, progressively, bit-by-bit, unfolds His nature and character to us.

Hebrews 1:1-3 says, "God, after He spoke long ago to the fathers in the prophets in many portions and in many ways, in these last days has spoken to us in His Son…" Many portions…Over the course of approximately 1800 years – from Job to Nehemiah – God wrote the Old Testament in 39 different portions. Many ways…These included visions, symbols, and parables, written in poetry and prose. This included different literary styles, but it was clearly always God's revelation of what He wanted His people to know. Culturally speaking, only one biblical author was a non-Jew. Humanly speaking, this is a Jewish book! How did the Jewish Culture understand the phrase, *Last days?* They understood the *last days* to be the time when the Messiah would come. Since Jesus, the Messiah, came, it has been the *last days.* So, when Jesus Christ came, God spoke the message of redemption, in fulfillment of His *thesis statement,* through His Son. This is beginning with the assumption that God exists and then, through *progressive revelation,* bit-by-bit unfolding His nature and character to His people, while advancing the actualization of His *thesis statement* in Genesis 3:15.

Even the name of God, *Jehovah,* reverberates this fact. When God commissioned Moses to go talk to Pharaoh and lead His people out of slavery, Moses had a question. In Exodus 3:13 Moses said, "Behold I am going to the sons of Israel, and I will say to them, The God of your fathers has sent me to you. Now they may say to me, what is His name? What shall I say to them?" In Exodus 3:14 God answered. "God said to Moses, I AM WHO I AM; and He said, thus you shall say to the sons of Israel, I AM has sent me to you." What in the world must Moses have thought? "I am…what? I am…who? Is there more information?" God preempted those thoughts and said, "I AM WHO I AM." In other words, there's nothing and no one to compare to Me. I just AM! The name *Jehovah* is a compound Hebrew word made up from the conjunction of 3 other Hebrew words that are all past, present, and future, tenses of the verb *to be,* or *I AM.*

Explain YHWH

All time begins in the future

So, He is the God Who always was, is now, and always will be! You see, as finite creatures, we can't think of time without thinking of it in its 3 tenses – past, present, and future. Further, all time begins in the future! In other words, there has never been a moment in time that was not *first* (at least in our finite minds) *future!* Swim in that one for a while! God created chronological time to accommodate our finite minds. We simply cannot think outside the realm of *time.* Being infinite in His existence, such tenses of time do not apply to God. That's why time is a gift to us from God!

The early church Father, Augustine of Hippo, wrote about this in the Third Century. Augustine concluded that time begins with the beginning of the universe. He made a sharp cut between the things that exist in time and space and what is outside time and space. Augustine began with the question 'What was God doing before He created Heaven and Earth?' and decided that the question has no meaning because words such as 'before' and 'after' and 'then' can't apply where time, as we know it, doesn't exist." Someone asked, "What was God doing before He created the universe?" Answer? Nothing! He didn't have time! According to Augustine, time as we know it is part and parcel of this creation, not something that applies to God. So, Augustine, astutely, described Him as "The God Who lives in the eternal present." 8

This same eternal attribute applies to Jesus Christ, as the second member of the Trinity. Seven times in the gospel of John, Jesus uses the "I Am" statement. Now, remember, John's purpose statement in John 20:30-31. Is it any wonder why John quoted Jesus in His diatribe with the Scribes and Pharisees in John 8:56-59? "Your father, Abraham, rejoiced to see My day, and he saw it and was glad. So, the Jews said to Him, 'You are not yet fifty years old, and have you seen Abraham?' Jesus said to them, truly, truly, I say to you, before Abraham was born, I am." The next verse says, "Therefore, they picked up stones to throw at Him, but Jesus hid Himself and went out of the temple." Why did they seek to immediately stone Jesus? They (the Jews) were very clear on His use of the verb "I AM". They knew Jesus was claiming to be God, and they considered it blasphemy! This is the God Who always was, is now, and always will be. This is the God Who lives in the eternal present, who is laying down His Redemptive Thesis Statement of Genesis 3:15! What is your choice to believe?

Chapter 11 God's Mission Strategy from Creation

Most Christians believe that God's strategy for reaching the world began with the Great Commission in Matthew 28:16-20. In reality, the work of the church is *Missions,* and God has been on *mission* since the opening chapter of His divine revelation to men, in Genesis. Websters 1828 Dictionary defines *Mission* as follows: "From the Latin *missio, from mitto, to send.* A sending or being sent, usually the latter; a being sent or delegated by authority, with certain powers for transacting business; commission; as sent on a foreign *mission.* Persons sent; any number of persons appointed by authority to perform any service; particularly, the persons sent to propagate religion, or evangelize the heathen. The societies for propagating the gospel have missions in almost every country. We have domestic missions and foreign missions." The last sentence in Webster's definition does not apply to the church. You will find no separation of *missions* into the categories of *domestic* and *foreign* in the Bible! Then, where did such categories come from? Not God! The Bible teaches, equips us for, and commands every believer to be engaged in *missions.* There are no exceptions. There are no exclusions. There are no exemptions. Nobody is left out!

> **The killer B's of the church are; buildings, bodies, budgets and bulletins**

Listen to a quote from Bruce Hunt, the renowned Missionary to Korea affiliated with the Orthodox Presbyterian Church for 48 years before going to be with the Lord in 1992. He said, "The work of the church is missions; That is, the work of the church is not primarily self-preservation, the perfection of organization and equipment, the improvement of the membership, nor several other firsts that people might propose. First, and foremost, the church is about mission before the church is about anything else. That is why we exist! That is who we are! We are a people on mission." We seem to be overwhelmingly confused about this. Many, if not most, believe the church is about buildings, bodies, budgets, and bulletins – what I call the "Killer B's". Many, if not the overwhelming majority of Pastors, subscribe to this belief. So, everything is programmed to facilitate this agenda; everything is for the building up of physical plant, numbers of people in the seats, and budgets required to fund this agenda and program. Some are willing to alter the tone of their preaching to assure this agenda is advanced. They take community surveys wherein they ask "Unchurched Harry" what would attract him to a church. Then they build in programming to accommodate his desires! Such unbiblical tactics for building numbers gives Satan a vote in directing the work of the Kingdom! These leaders believe that the church must have a perpetual "Building Program" to be seen as *moving forward* (whatever that means in Madison Avenue strategies). Therefore, they have an ever-present *Building Fund* to build athletic facilities, Coffee Houses, and such things as you will never find an example of, nor a whisper about, in the New Testament!

> **The teaching of the Bible is replete with teaching on *Justice*, but there's no adjective preceding that word**

Yet others subscribe to the idea that the mission of the church is to be the purveyor of the *Social Gospel*. These will go as far as to say, "If your preaching of the Gospel of Jesus Christ does not include the preaching of *Social Justice*, then you are not preaching the Gospel of Jesus Christ!" Search the scriptures from Genesis 1:1 to Revelation 22:21 and you will not find a line that supports such! The Apostle Paul wrote the lion's share of the New Testament. He ministered in *hotbeds* of *Social Injustice*. In fact, during the era of Paul's ministry the Roman Empire was in control of most of the known world. In his *Antiquities,* Flavius Josephus estimates that, at that time, roughly one third of the population of the known world were slaves! In spite of this fact nowhere do you find in Paul's writings a departure from the Gospel of Jesus Christ, and the tenants of faith, to focus on *Social Justice!* The teaching of the Bible is replete with teaching on *Justice,* but there's no adjective preceding that word! Despite this, in many churches, preaching of the Gospel of Jesus Christ and Justice, as found in the scriptures, has given way to the heralding of *Social Justice!* The Apostle Paul ministered in places that were absolutely social train wrecks. For example, in Corinth, there was the Temple of Dianna at the pinnacle of the city, with its temple prostitutes numbering in the thousands. These women were *slaves* to the religious establishment that managed the worship of the pagan deity! Yet, neither letter to the church at Corinth mentions this, but instead, teaches the truths of Jesus Christ to the believers, and addresses their sin. At the bottom of the hill at Corinth, there was the Temple of Apollos, which was devoted to homosexuality. Neither of Paul's letters to the church at Corinth makes any mention of this, but sticks to the critical matter of doctrine and duty for the believers. Paul's teaching at Corinth included matters of *Justice,* but there was no adjective preceding the word! In the contemporary church of today, you find scarce preaching on doctrine, duty, sin, and the glory of God. These topics are considered *irrelevant* in the face of our society, which promotes strife, reverse-racism, Marxism, identity politics, and intersectionality. The message must not offend anyone – no matter how counter to God's word the behavior, speech, ideology, or activity. However, *Social Justice,* as it is the hot button of Western culture, dominates the message coming across the pulpit!

While these versions of *consumer-friendly* Christianity proliferate in the West, especially in America, these are not in the same hemisphere with the work of the church! The work of the church is

Missions! God has always been on mission, and it is the work of His Body, the church.

The Sons of Promise

We have biblically identified God's mission for the church. Now, we will trace how God provided, protected, and advanced His process of providing *the seed of the woman* promised to man in His thesis statement in Genesis 3:15 through the *Sons of Promise*.

In Genesis 5 we find a genealogy from Adam to Noah. We typically skip over this chapter, as reading it is about as interesting as watching paint dry. We have the repetition of the statement that says *this person lived so many years and became the father of that person. Then this person lived so many years after he fathered that person and he had other sons and daughters, and he died.* Genesis 5:1-5 begins thus, "This is the book of the generations of Adam. In the day when God created man, He made him in the likeness of God. He created them male and female, and He blessed them and named them Man in the day when they were created. When Adam had lived one hundred and thirty years, he became the father of a son in his own image, and named him Seth. Then the days of Adam after he became the father of Seth were eight hundred years, and he had other sons and daughters. So, all the days that Adam lived were nine hundred and thirty years, and he died." Genesis 5 reads like that through 6 generations until we get to Enoch. Enoch's life doesn't end the same way. Genesis 5:21-24 says "Enoch lived sixty-five years, and became the father of Methuselah. Then Enoch walked with God three hundred years after he became the father of Methuselah, and he had other sons and daughters. So, all the days of Enoch were three hundred and sixty-five years. Enoch walked with God; and he was not, for God took him."

Usually when we read this chapter, we focus on the two *exceptional* people and forget about the rest. The first one we usually focus on is

Methuselah because the Bible places him as the oldest man who ever lived at 969 years of age. Next, we focus on Enoch as exceptional because the Bible tells us that he walked with God and he never died since God *took him.* There are some interesting and helpful things we can learn about God, and about ourselves, by studying these two men. That's for another time, and maybe even another book. However, the main purpose of Genesis 5 is not to highlight the lives of these two men. Genesis 5 is the genealogy of how we got from Adam to Noah. There are seven generations from Adam through Enoch. They are: Adam, Seth, Enosh, Kenan, Mahalalel, Jared, and Enoch. Enoch's offspring, listed by name, is Methuselah. Methuselah's offspring, listed by name, is Lamech. Lamech's offspring, listed by name is, is Noah. Notice, though each man named had "many other sons and daughters" over a period of 100's of years, we're not given all of those names. For example, we know that Adam and Eve had two sons prior to Seth. Why is Seth mentioned, by name, while there's no mention of Cain and Able? The reason is, those mentioned by name (such as Seth) are crucial in preservation of the "Seed of the woman" promised in God's thesis statement of Genesis 3:15!

If you trace the *Sons of Promise* through Noah (11 generations) you have Ham, Shem, and Japheth in Genesis 5:32. All 3 of Noah's sons appear by name in Genesis chapters 5-11. So, which one of them is the *Son of Promise?* I'm glad you asked! In Genesis 11:10 we begin to read about the descendants of Shem. Genesis 11 appears in the same format as the genealogy in Genesis 5. However, Shem's genealogy extends through Terah, who became the father, of Abram. Here, we learn that Shem is the *Son of Promise* through whom runs the lineage of the Messiah through Abram! Abram's (which means *exalted father in Hebrew)* name was changed by God to *Abraham* (Genesis 17:5), which means *father of many.* Abraham became the father of Ishmael and Isaac. Ishmael, born to Abraham not through his wife, Sarah, but through her handmaid, Hagar, was 14 years older than Isaac. In Genesis 17:18 Abraham pleaded with God to accept Ishmael as the one through whom God would keep His covenant with Abraham to provide him with *Land (Genesis 12:1), Seed (Genesis 12:2), and the Messiah (Genesis 12:3).* God rejected Abraham's request. Genesis 17:19 says, "But God said, No, but Sarah your wife will bear you a son, and you shall call his name Isaac: and I will establish My covenant with him for an everlasting covenant for his descendants after him." Isaac is identified as the *Son of Promise,* through whom would be the lineage of the Messiah (the seed of the woman)/. Isaac fathered Jacob (Genesis 25:26), whom God selected as the *Son of Promise* over his elder brother, Esau.

> **So, the story of Joseph is actually about *Jacob*! It is *not* about Joseph!**

Jacob had 12 sons, who became the patriarchs of the 12 Tribes of Israel. Of these 12 sons we would probably, humanly, think that Joseph is identified as the *Son of Promise* because of his *rags to power and riches* story. We are biblically, humanly and horribly wrong! In Genesis 37, we read, "These are the Generations of Jacob." So, since that is one of the key ways that the book of Genesis is divided, by *Generations,* we know that this narrative is *not* primarily to highlight Joseph. Moses tells us, very clearly in Genesis 37:2, that "In this part of Genesis (boys and girls) I'm talking about...Jacob!" So, the story of Joseph occurs *within* the narrative of the story of Jacob. So, the story of Joseph is actually about *Jacob*! It is *not* about Joseph! He is not the main character in this movie! He is a character that we are to take special note of, because he is a "type" of Christ. However, he is not the *main* character in this story! We look at him so that we can understand the story of Jacob! This is Jacob's narrative. Jacob is one of the *Sons of*

Promise. If you understand that, then you understand that the focus of Genesis 37- 41 is not that it is *Joseph's* story. Jacob's narrative tells us about how God preserved and advanced the coming of The Seed of the woman" (Genesis 3:15), and identifies for us the next in the succession of the *Sons of Promise*.

In Genesis 44, Judah has offered himself in the place of Benjamin. This offer of substitution identifies Judah as the *Son of Promise*. Up to this point, we didn't know which of Jacob's sons would be the *Son of Promise*. So, Judah is the new head of the family. Remember the promise made by God in Genesis 3:15; The Promised Seed is going to come through a particular blood line. Is it Ishmael? No, It's Isaac. Is it Esau? No, it is Jacob. Now, Jacob has 12 sons, so which one is it? There's only one line that can bring us the Messiah. Jacob has a favorite son in Joseph, but Joseph is not the *Son of Promise*. Who is? Judah is the *Son of Promise* and he's identified by offering himself in the place of the Son Whom His Father loves. Does that sound familiar?

You see, Judah's going to have a *greater son* who does something very similar. Ahhh …. don't go too far. I'm talking about *David!* David comes to prominence in Israel when he volunteered to go out to fight Goliath. He went to that battle as a *substitute representative* of the people of God into a valley to fight their foe; He defeats their foe, thereby winning victory for all of the people that are 'in him'. Does *that* sound familiar? Put together what Judah did and what David did and you have their *greater Son, Jesus,* who goes down into valley of the shadow of death, offers Himself as a substitute for the brothers whom His Father loves, defeats their foe, and therein wins victory for all of those who are 'in Him'! There's the gospel!

In Genesis 44:18-33 Judah is identified as the *Son of Promise,* as he offers himself as a substitute for Benjamin. At this point, we can leap to the ultimate *Son of Promise – the seed of the woman!*

Revelations 5:5 calls Jesus Christ "...the Lion of the Tribe of Judah."

> **God employed and deployed the *Sons of Promise*, and their flawed progeny, to the advancement of the fulfillment of His promise to provide *the seed of the woman, His Messiah!***

You can trace the Messiah's lineage from there in Matthew 1 (through His adoptive father, Joseph), and Luke 3 (through his mother, Mary). The genealogy goes from them (Joseph and Mary), through David, back to Judah! In Luke 2:10,11, an Angel of the Lord first proclaimed His virgin birth to lowly shepherds. The angel said, "...do not be afraid; for behold, I bring you good news (literally, *good message – gospel* in Greek) of great joy which will be for *all the people*; for today in the city of David there has been born for you a Savior, who is *Christ* the Lord" (emphasis mine). In his use of the title *Christ,* we find the Greek rendering of the title *Messiah.* This is the Son that God promised back in Genesis 3:15 – *the seed of the woman!* Only through *"the seed of the woman"* could God's promise in Genesis 12:3 be fulfilled. There, God promised Abraham that "...in you all the families of the earth will be blessed." Through Messiah Jesus, and only through Him, are all families of the earth blessed! It is only through Messiah Jesus that the greatest blessing available to mankind (being made right with God) is made available to mankind! God employed and deployed the *Sons of Promise*, and their flawed progeny, to the advancement of the fulfillment of His promise to provide *the seed of the woman, His Messiah!* Through the *Sons of Promise,* He gave us His Ultimate *Son of Promise,* the promised *seed of the woman.* Galatians 3:16 says, "Now the promises were spoken to Abraham and to his seed. He does not say, "and to seeds," as referring to many, but rather to one. And to your seed, that is, Christ." It is because of the work of this One, promised *Seed, Promised Messiah,* that we who believe and trust in Jesus Christ are now what the Bible calls Abraham's *descendants* (Galatians 4:16), and Abraham's *children* (Galatians 3:7)! We are the *Sons of Promise* through whom God has determined to bring the offer of the blessing to "all families of the earth!" This was all set-in motion when, simultaneous with *the curse* God promised *the seed of the woman and the work that He would do to redeem us!* This is the Ultimate Son of Promise – the Lord Jesus Christ!

At the very beginning, immediately after the fall of man, God promised the deliverer – *The Seed of the Woman, the ultimate Son of Promise, the Lord Jesus Christ!* He would be the One Who would do everything necessary to restore Man to a right relationship with God. He is 100% God and 100% Man, and yet, He is only 100%. He is as much *God* as if He'd never been *Man,* and as much *Man* as if He'd never been *God.* He came in the likeness of sinful man to show us what God is like and what Man *should* be like. Bigger than that, He came into His creation to offer Himself as the innocent *substitute* to pay for the sin of all who would trust in and rely solely on Him and what He has done, rather than on anything they themselves can do to be made right with God. This is the *good news!* This is the answer to the question of the ages. The most crucial, critical, personal, monumental question of the ages is *How can a man escape hell, be made right with God, and go to heaven?* The Isaiah 53 was written to answer this question. The book of Romans was written to answer this question. God's thesis statement in Genesis 3:15 was written to answer this question. The balance of the Bible was written to answer this question! Since faith in, trust in, full reliance upon, Jesus and what He has done is the answer, what then is the *method* God put in place for this *good news* to reach all men of all ages? I'm glad you asked! We will explore the depths of that next!

Chapter 12 God's Strategy for Spreading the Good News to All Men

> **We think about *Missions* as this sort of *New Testament* idea. Nothing is further from the truth!**

God's strategy for getting the good news of the gospel to all mankind is *missions*. When we think of *Missions*, the first thing that comes to mind is usually the Great Commission. As we said earlier, most Christians believe that God's strategy for reaching the world began with Matthew 28:16-20. We think about *Missions* as this sort of *New Testament* idea. Nothing is further from the truth! What we're going to start with is a survey of the concept, the strategy, of *Missions* in the Hebrew Bible, the Old Testament. For many Christians this is an oxymoron. They cannot conceive of *Missions* in the Old Testament. Why don't we see this? Most Christians have no idea that the foundation for God's strategy for reaching the world with the gospel is stated in Genesis 1:27-28. The text says, "God created man in His own image, in the image of God He created him; male and female He created them. God blessed them; and God said to them, Be fruitful and multiply, and fill the earth, and subdue it; and rule over the fish of the sea and over the birds of the sky and over every living thing that moves on the earth." Why have we missed this? Great question! There are actually several reasons that jump out at us when we critically examine this proposition from the scriptures. Here, we offer the following three reasons:

Fixation on the Great Commission

We're fixated on the Great Commission. What's really sad about this is that we have, by and large, from limited to no understanding of what the Great Commission is all about! Further, we believe that this, the Great Commission, found in Matthew 28:16-20, is the *Inauguration of Missions!* It is far from that. Additionally, we've turned the Great Commission into a *Foreign Missions text for those called to be Missionaries,* or we see it as an *evangelism* text. It is neither! By the way, you will not find a division between *foreign* and *home* missions in the scripture. Who invented that? God did not! Wherever the Savior has a *strategy* the enemy, Satan, has a *subtle substitute!* Unfortunately, the Church operates much more by *Satan's subtle substitute* than it does by the *Savior's strategy!* More on that later.

Dispensational Bias

Next, we've missed God's focus on *missions* throughout the Bible due to a *Dispensational* bias. The New Testament Greek word for "dispensation" (*Gr. oikonomia*) comes from two words, "house" (*oikos*) "law" (*nomos*), and refers to the oversight, management, economy, administration over a house or others' property. The word *oikonomia* is translated "dispensation" or "stewardship" in a number of verses in the New Testament (Luke 16:2–4; 1 Corinthians 9:17; Ephesians 3:2; Colossians 1:25). The the idea was that God functioned through the history of redemption in different ways. There is Biblical Dispensationalism as compared to Popular Dispensationalism.

For example, the old dispensations began with *Innocence.* In other words, there was a time before the fall when man was innocent. God mediated His rule on earth to man in an innocent condition and treated him as innocent. Then came sin, and you had *Conscience.* The dispensation of conscience meant God was working with man who now had a conscience that could tell right from wrong; that's why he made clothes, covered himself, hid in the garden – he had a guilty conscience.

Next, in order to control man, God brought in the next dispensation, which was *Human Government.* God ordained certain systems of government to control this sinful creation called *man* to keep him from totally destroying himself. This included the first criminal law, which was Capital Punishment; if a man takes a life, he must forfeit his own life as a penalty. There were other offenses that were to result in Capital Punishment. Capital Punishment would preserve the dignity of man and solidify and maintain the respect for the image of God in created men. Human government was then followed by the dispensation of *Law*.

This was followed by the dispensation of *Grace,* or the New Covenant. This is followed by the dispensation of the *Church*. This is followed by the dispensation of the *Kingdom*. This is followed by the dispensation of the *Eternal State* – the new heavens and the new earth. Someone figured out these seven dispensations and laid them out this way. There is nothing necessarily *inspired* about the layout. In the scripture, you can see God working with Adam before the fall (Innocence), and working with Adam after the fall (*Conscience*). You can search the scriptures and see God working with Moses before the cross, during the time of the *Law*. Scripture is crystal clear on God working after the cross through the *New Covenant* through grace in Christ. Currently, we are in the dispensation of the *church.* A thorough study of scripture reveals that God will, in the future, be working in the *Kingdom*. Finally, God will usher in the dispensation of the *Eternal State*, the new heaven and the new earth. We all can see that.

It's what you do with those categories that becomes problematic. Some of the old-fashioned dispensationalists made those categories hard and fast; they also assumed that God saved people different ways in different dispensations! There are still people who believed that there was no *Grace* in the Old Testament, and that there's no *Law* in the New Testament. It is not wrong to see that God operated in all those ways. It is wrong to make them hard and fast and invent different means of salvation and multiple covenants by which God saves; This cannot be supported with scripture! People who do this are generally referred to as *Hyper-Dispensationalists.* For example, these folks would look at the Beatitudes, in Matthew 5, and say, "Why do we care about that? That's part of the Sermon on the Mount, which is all about the Kingdom age – the Millennial Kingdom. We're not in that dispensation. We're in the dispensation of the Church. Accordingly, what Jesus taught is only relevant to His dispensation and the Kingdom to come when He returns. It says nothing about the Church." This Hyper-Dispensationalist view is the incubator of untold heresies. Campbellites were followers of Thomas and Alexander Campbell. This father/son team of unorthodox theologians invented aberrant beliefs like *baptismal regeneration* and the belief that Christians could unite to transform the world and initiate the Millennial Kingdom. These errors are directly the products Hyper-Dispensational theology. This madness dissects the Bible into little pieces, instead of seeing one mosaic from a panoramic view.

> **When God promised to give a kingdom to the nation of Israel that is not a synonym for the Church.**

It is not difficult to cut it straight. 2 Timothy 3:16 says, "All scripture is breathed out by God and profitable for teaching, for reproof, for correction, and for training in righteousness." In other words, when God says *Israel,* He means *Israel,* not the Church. When God promised to give a kingdom to the nation of Israel that is not a synonym for the Church. To have the Biblical viewpoint of *dispensations,* all we need to do is maintain the distinction between the nation of Israel and the Church, and see the continuity between the Old Covenant and the New Covenant. There is grace in the Old Testament and there is law in the New Testament. Genesis 6:8 says, "But Noah found grace in the eyes of the LORD." Genesis 15:6 says, "Abraham believed God and it was counted to him as righteousness." During the dispensation of *Law,* as during the dispensation of *Grace,* salvation has *always* been by grace through faith! The continuity between the testaments is staggering, and any study of God's word is deficient in the absence of that fact always being the backdrop! Unfortunately, most Christians have been indoctrinated to ignore this fact, or even dispute it. Therefore, most of us have been indoctrinated with a hardline dispensational bias and miss the prevalence of missions in the Old Testament.

The Tanakh - Old Covenant

Next, there is a definitive lack of familiarity with the text – the Old Covenant. Many Christians have no familiarity with what we call the Old Covenant and what God was doing there. I will go as far as to say this applies to *most* Christians! One of my beloved siblings, a professing Christian, said, "Why are you always referencing and incorporating the Old Testament in your teaching. I do not live under the Law! I'm under grace!" What a tragic misunderstanding of both terms, Law and Grace! Because the typical Christian has never been taught how the testaments connect and harmonize, there is a hefty crater in his/her understanding of the word of God. Jesus, the Apostles, and the early church taught the gospel from the only scriptures they had available to them - the Old Covenant.

In 1 Corinthians 15:3-4 Paul wrote, "For I delivered to you as of first Importance what I also received, that Christ died for our sins according to the scriptures, and that He was buried, and that He was raised on the third day according to the scriptures." In Romans 16:25-27 Paul wrote, "Now to Him who is able to establish you according to my gospel and the preaching of Jesus Christ, according to the revelation of the mystery, which has been kept secret for long ages past, but now is manifested, and by the scriptures of the prophets, according to the commandment of the eternal God, has been made known to all the nations, leading to obedience of faith; to the only wise God, through Jesus Christ, be glory forever, Amen." One cannot understand the second coming of Christ without studying Daniel. Lastly, It is impossible to understand at least 90% of the New Testament book of Hebrews without the Tanakh. My Discipler, Herb Hodges, routinely said, "The Old Covenant is Christianity in embryo. The New Covenant Is Christianity full grown and full blown."

The Old Covenant is vital to our understanding of the God of the universe. Hebrews 1:1-4 reads as follows: "God after He spoke long ago to the fathers in the prophets in many portions and in many ways, in these last days has spoken to us in His Son, whom He appointed heir of all things, through whom also He made the world. And He is the radiance of His glory and the exact representation of His nature, and upholds all things by the word of His power, when He had made purification of sins, He sat down at the right hand of the Majesty on high, having become as much better than the angels, as He has Inherited a more excellent name than they." This passage describes *progressive revelation.* The infinite God bit-by-bit unfolded His nature and character to man, because of man's finite limitations of understanding.

Not one of the Old Covenant Prophets had a full-orbed understanding of the nature and character of God. Isaiah saw His holiness. Jeremiah saw His forgiveness. Amos saw His justice. Therefore, God spoke in *many portions.* Over the course of approximately 1,800 years (from Job, 2200 B.C.) to Nehemiah (400 B.C.) the Old Covenant was written in 39 different books reflecting different historical times, locations, cultures, and situations. During this time, He spoke in *many ways.* These included visions, symbols, and parables, written in both poetry and prose. The progressive revelation of the Old Covenant described God's plan of redemption for man.

1 Peter 1:10-11 says, "As to this salvation, the prophets who prophesied of the grace that would come to you made careful searches and inquiries, seeking to know what person or time the Spirit of Christ within them was indicating as He predicted the sufferings of Christ and the glories to follow." This *progressive revelation* in the Old Covenant also spoke of God's will for His people. In Romans 15:4 we read, "For whatever was written in earlier times was written for our instruction, so that through perseverance and the encouragement of the scriptures we might have hope."

> **That is because Jesus is 100% God, as well as being 100% man; yet He is only 100%! He is as much *God* as if He had *never* been *man*, and as much *man* as if He had *never* been God.**

God's final speech about, and revelation of, His nature and character is detailed in Hebrews 1:2, where we read, "...in these last days has spoken in His Son..." In the person of Jesus Christ, we see what God *is* like, and what man *should be* like. That is because Jesus is 100% God, as well as being 100% man; yet He is only 100%! He is as much *God* as if He had *never* been *man*, and as much *man* as if He had *never* been God. John 1:18 says, "No one has seen God at any time; the only begotten God (Jesus) who is in the bosom of the Father, He has explained Him." Therefore, Jesus picked up explaining (literally *spelled God out* in Greek) the nature and character of God where the Old Covenant left off. Again, it is impossible to have any semblance of a detailed grasp of the nature and character of the Father or the Son without thorough study of the Old Covenant - described, unwittingly, by many Christians as "The Law". In the next chapter, we will clarify "The Law".

Chapter 13 Three Facets of Biblical Law

There are three different facets of Biblical Law; Moral, Ceremonial, and Judicial/Civil.

Moral Law

The moral laws, or (Hebrew) *mishpatim*, relate to justice and judgment and are often translated as "ordinances." *Mishpatim* are said to be based on God's holy nature. As such, the ordinances are holy, just, and unchanging. Their purpose is to promote the welfare of those who obey. The value of the laws is considered obvious by reason and common sense. The moral law encompasses regulations on justice, respect, and sexual conduct, and includes the Ten Commandments. It also includes penalties for failure to obey the ordinances. The Moral and Ceremonial Law lead people to Christ.

Modern Protestants are divided over the applicability of *mishpatim* in the church age. Some believe that Jesus' assertion that the law will remain in effect until all is accomplished (Matthew 5:18) means that believers are still bound to it. This is the proper, orthodox view of the moral law. In other words, "thou shall not kill" applies to me, as a Christian, or anyone else, as strongly as it applied to any Old Testament Israelite.

Others, like my sibling, misinterpret that Jesus fulfilled this requirement (Matthew 5:17), and that we are instead under the law of Christ (Galatians 6:2), which is thought to be "love God and love others" (Matthew 22:36-40). Jesus did not "abolish" the moral law in the sense of eliminating it. In Hebrew, the word *Kaim* meant to abolish. When a person interpreted the law incorrectly, the Rabbis described this as *abolishing* the law. In other words, if a person followed your erroneous interpretation, they would not be keeping the law, but they would be disobeying as if the law didn't exist. By contrast, the Hebrew word for *fulfill* is *Botel*. This word means to correctly interpret the law. It does not mean to simply obey the law. In Matthew 5:17, Jesus said, "Do not think that I came to abolish the Law or the Prophets; I did not come to abolish but to fulfill." The phrase "Law or the Prophets" is another way of referring to what we call the Old Testament. The *law* deals with precepts and principles concerning conduct. The *prophets* provide prophecies concerning Christ. Jesus said that He came to correctly interpret (Botel) the scriptures so that men might obey God. That is very different from the idea that Jesus kept the whole law, He fulfilled it in that way for me because He knew that I couldn't keep it perfectly; therefore, I'm not under the law, but under grace and the law of love. No! Five times in Matthew 5:21-43 Jesus said, "You have heard that it was said...but I say unto you..." This is another way of saying, in effect, "Your Rabbis taught you this, but I am correcting (Botel) their faulty interpretation (Kaim) in order that you can obey God."

One easy way to think of the Christian's obligation to the *Moral Law* is this: I am *not* under the Law as far as it's penalties and its punishment, and I shall never be. Jesus Christ took that for me and nailed it to His cross. However, I *am* under the Law as far as it's precepts and its principles are concerned. In other words, "Thou shall not steal" applies to every Christian just as much as it did any Old Testament Israelite, and all other human beings!

Martin Luther said it this way, "The law is a mirror, a hammer, and a whip. It is a mirror to hold up in front of you so that you can see your true condition before God. It is a hammer to smash your self-confidence (reliance on self), and it is a whip to drive you to Christ!"

Ceremonial Law

The ceremonial laws are called *hukkim* or *chuqqah* in Hebrew, which literally means "custom of the nation"; the words are often translated as "statutes." These laws seem to focus the adherent's attention on God. They include instructions on regaining right standing with God (e.g., sacrifices and other ceremonies regarding "uncleanness"), remembrances of God's work in Israel (e.g., feasts and festivals), specific regulations meant to distinguish Israelites from their pagan neighbors (e.g., dietary and clothing restrictions), and signs that point to the coming Messiah (e.g., the Sabbath, circumcision, Passover, and the redemption of the firstborn). Some Jews believe that the ceremonial law is not fixed. They hold that, as societies evolve, so do God's expectations of how his followers should relate to Him. This view is not in harmony with the Bible. God is immutable, meaning that He never changes. James 1:17 says, "Every good thing given and every perfect gift is from above, coming down from the Father of lights, with whom there is no variation or shifting shadow." Hebrews 13:8 harmonizes this. It says, "Jesus Christ *is* the same yesterday and today, and forever." God never changes! He does, however, use certain things long enough to fulfill His purposes. When such purposes are fulfilled, those things cease. It is not that God changed His mind; He never intended for those things to be permanent!

> **Nowhere in the New Testament are Christians commanded to keep the Sabbath**

Ceremonial law does not bind Christians. Since the church is not the nation of Israel, memorial festivals, such as the Feast of Weeks and Passover, do not apply.

There is still debate in protestant churches over the applicability of the Sabbath, and there should not be. God's word on how the Sabbath should be handled by Christians is not ambiguous! Some say that its inclusion in the Ten Commandments gives it the weight of moral law. Others quote Colossians 2:16-17 and Romans 14:5 to explain that Jesus has fulfilled the Sabbath and become our Sabbath rest. First, Colossians 2:16-17 says, "Therefore, no one is to act as your judge in regard to food and drink, or in respect to a festival or a new moon, or a Sabbath day, things which are a shadow of what is to come; but the substance belongs to Christ." That the Apostle Paul includes the Sabbath Day observance among those *shadows* that God commanded of the Israelites that are not binding on Christians should be sufficient to settle the matter. Nowhere in the New Testament are Christians commanded to keep the Sabbath. In Acts 15, when the great Jerusalem Council, consisting of all of the Apostles and leaders of the Jerusalem Church, met to determine what edicts to hand down to Gentile congregations, the keeping of the Sabbath was not included. The Sabbath was not observed by the Patriarchs, i.e., Abraham, Isaac, and Jacob. Romans 14:5 says, "Each one should be fully convinced in his own mind." Romans 14:5 is the primary passage on the matter of how individual Christians should not violate their conscience.

The conscience is the doorway to the influence of the Holy Spirit. A continual violation of one's conscience leads to the conscience being *seared*. For example, when you burn yourself deeply enough to *sear* the flesh, that area no longer retains the same degree of sensitivity. The same is true when one repeatedly violates the conscience. When this happens, the conscience is no longer sensitive to the impetus of the Holy Spirit. This passage has nothing at all to do with whether one is to obey the Moral Law! The applicability of the Law in the life of a Christian has always related to its usefulness in loving God, and loving others. These are the two distinct *tables* of the Law. The first three of the Ten Commandments deal with loving God. The six commandments at the end deal with loving your neighbor. The Sabbath Law, number four, in the Ten Commandments, is the *sign* of the covenant. A *sign* marked every covenant God gave. The sign of the Abrahamic Covenant was *circumcision*. The sign of the Noahic Covenant was the *rainbow*. The sign of the Ten

Commandments is the *Sabbath Law*. It is, therefore, not morally binding.

Galatians 3:24 says, "Therefore the law has become our tutor to lead us to Christ, that we may be justified by faith." The Greek word for *tutor,* is paidagogos. In the New Testament world this was a slave employed by Greek or Roman families, whose job it was to supervise young boys for their parents. They took them to and from school, made sure they studied their lessons, and taught them obedience. They were strict disciplinarians that scolded and whipped as whatever punishment they saw fit. The role of the paidagogos was never permanent, and it was a great celebration when a boy finally gained freedom from his paidagogos. His purpose was to take care of the child only until he grew into adulthood. At that time the relationship radically changed. The two of them might remain friendly, but the paidagogos had no more authority over the young man. The sole purpose of the Law, God's divinely appointed paidagogos, was to lead men to Christ, that they might be justified. After a person come to Him, there is no longer need for the external ceremonies and rituals to act as guides and disciplinarians, because the new inner principles operate through the indwelling Christ, in whom is "hidden all the treasures of wisdom and knowledge" – Colossians 2:3. The law in the ceremonial sense is done away with, though in the moral sense it remains always an intimate friend that one seeks to love and favor.

Judicial/Civil Law

The Westminster Confession adds the category of judicial or civil law. These laws were specifically given for the culture and place of the Israelites and encompass all of the moral law except the Ten Commandments. This includes everything from murder to restitution for a man gored by an ox and the responsibility of the man who dug a pit to rescue his neighbor's trapped donkey (Exodus

21:12-36). Since the Jews saw no difference between their God-ordained morality and their cultural responsibilities, this category is used by Christians far more than by Jewish scholars. The division of the Jewish law into different categories is a human construct designed to better understand the nature of God and define which laws church-age Christians are still required to follow. *All* the law is useful for instruction (2 Timothy 3:16). Christians are not under the law (Romans 10:4). Ephesians 2:15–16 says, "…by abolishing in His flesh the enmity, *which is* the Law of commandments *contained* in ordinances, so that in Himself He might make the two into one new man, *thus* establishing peace, and might reconcile them both in one body to God through the cross, by it having put to death the enmity." Jesus fulfilled the law, thus abolishing the difference between Jew and Gentile. God does not have two peoples! He has one people that makes up the one body; this happens when any individual Jew or any individual Gentile places his/her faith in Jesus Christ and what He has done, rather than in anything they, themselves, can do. It is critical that the Christian truly understand the purpose and meaning of the law in scripture; it is equally important that we understand the purpose and scope of the different divisions of law.

Now that we've clarified *truth,* the critical necessity of the *Old Covenant*, and the meaning of *the Law,* in the following chapters we can expose God's plan for fulfilling His prophecy concerning *the seed of the woman.*

Missions In the Old Covenant

Let us begin our survey of missions in the Old Covenant (Tanakh) by looking at a New Testament passage, Matthew 23:15. You ask, "How are we going to begin a survey of Old Testament passages on this subject when we're starting in the New Testament?" I'm glad you asked! At the time this portion of Matthew's narrative speaks to, Jesus had not yet been crucified and resurrected, which ushered in and established the New Covenant (another expression for New Testament). Therefore, technically, those believers of this time, including the Apostles, were *Old Testament* Saints in transition. Therefore, we want to begin by looking at how these *Old Testament* believers, of Jesus' day, viewed *missions.* The text says, "Woe to you, Scribes and Pharisees, hypocrites, because you travel around on sea and land to make one proselyte; and when he becomes one, you make him twice as much a son of hell as yourselves." Why would these "us four – no more – shut the door" Scribes and Pharisees travel across land and sea to make converts? That's missions! Where would the Pharisees even get the idea? How did you have Gentiles converting to Judaism? They got it from the Hebrew Bible – the Old Testament, which contains a vigorous *mission* mindset!

Chapter 14 Missions in the Pentateuch

God's Dominion Mandate

First, there's the *Dominion Mandate* in Genesis 1:27-28. This text says, "God created man in His own image, in the image of God He created him; male and female He created them. God blessed them; and God said to them, 'Be fruitful and multiply and fill the earth, and subdue it; and rule over the fish of the sea and over the birds of the sky and over every living thing that moves on the earth.'" That is *Missions.*

At this point, it would be proper for us to set forth the Biblical definition of *Missions.* We previously gave Merriam-Webster's definition of *Missions.* The Biblical definition of Missions is "One with consummate authority – the Master - commanding the sending of His subordinate – slave, at a specific time, to a specific area, to perform a specific task, according to specific instructions, for a specified outcome. The slave is endowed with the resources and authority of the Master. The slave has no will, rights, resources, nor schedule of his own. The will of the Master dominates his heart. The slave's charge is simply to obey the Master!"

This definition of *missions* is based on the Great Commission as found in Matthew 28:16-20. It tells us *who, when, what, where, how, and why.* In verse 18 Jesus said, "All authority in heaven and earth (the only realms we know exists) is given to Me." That is consummate authority; that is the *why* we are to obey His commands. Verse 19 says, "Go therefore, and make disciples of all nations..." The word *Go* is a present circumstantial participle. It means *as you are going, or since you are going.* The word *you* (2nd person plural) is implied. So, this tells us *who* is to be involved. Who is that? YOU! HIS SLAVE! It also tells us the specific *when* we are to obey the command; "as you are going" means NOW...ALWAYS! It is not a command, but modifies the command to *make disciples.* These two phrases give the specific time and specific task to be accomplished. Then verse 19 says that we, His slaves, are to make disciples of *"all nations."* This tells us *what* we are to do, and *where* we are to do it. Verse 19 goes on to say, "…baptizing them in the name of the Father, and in the name of the Son, and in the name of the Holy Ghost, and teaching them (those disciples) to obey all that I've commanded you." These constitute specific instructions on *how* to perform the task of making disciples.

You say, OK, Jim. There's one part of the definition missing. Where is the reference to *slaves* in the Great Commission? I'm glad you asked. That's found in the plural pronoun "you" that is gleaned from the original Greek text. This tells us *who* Jesus is commanding; Jesus is talking to all of His *slaves.* You may say, "Well, I don't see the word *slave or slaves* in this text." No, you don't physically see that word, but it's there.

> **Paul said that this is the way we Christians should want people to think of us; we should want that they should think of us as that *strapped-in galley slave* in the bottom of the ship!**

In 1 Corinthians 4:1 Paul writes, "Let a man so account of us, as the ministers of Christ, and stewards of the mysteries of God." The word translated *ministers* is the Greek word *huperetes.* This word means *under-oarsman,* or an *under-rower.* It is the word for a strapped-in *galley slave* pulling his oar, with all of his strength, on command from the *Cadence Captain,* in the bottom of the boat! He has no will of his own, no rights of his own, no schedule of his own, no resources of his own. He doesn't know where the ship is going. He has to be told when the ship has arrived. He never leaves the ship alive, but is carried out dead! That *slave* has one focus; he must move his oar in sync with all the other *under-rowers,* not by watching them, but by keeping his whole attention on that Cadence Captain! Paul said that this is the way we Christians should want people to think of us; we should want that they should think of us as that *strapped-in galley slave* in the bottom of the ship! This is only one example of how the Bible describes the followers of Jesus as His *slaves!*

You say, "Now wait Jim. Those are the words of Paul and not the words of Jesus. Jesus' words are in red! Remember 2 Timothy 3:16? "All scripture is breathed out by God"! If you have a Bible with the words spoken by Jesus in red, please understand that the words not in red are equally important because they represent the very words of God! Therefore, when Jesus gave the Great Commission, and says "Go", or *as you are going, or since you are going,* He was talking to His *slaves!* The Biblical definition of *Missions* is "One with consummate authority – the Master - commanding the sending of His subordinate – *slave,* at a specific time, to a specific area, to perform a specific task, according to specific instructions, for a specified outcome. The slave is endowed with the resources and authority of the Master. The slave has no will, rights, schedule, nor resources of his own. The will of the Master dominates his heart. The slave's charge is simply to obey the Master!" By this definition (not Websters) God has always been on *Mission!* We will explore this in-depth later.

Right now, we continue our survey in the Old Testament. God's (the Master) focus on Missions is substantiated in His command to Adam to fill the earth (specific time, area, task, instructions, and outcome) with those made in His image – with His *image bearers!* Because of his imminent death, and the eventual death of each succeeding generation, Adam's progeny would need to be taught *Who* God is, *What* God has done, *How* He made the world, and *What* His mandate is. In other words, in order for God's *mission* to be advanced *in all the earth* the command had to be passed to, and followed by, Adam's progeny.

God gave His *Dominion Mandate* to man right at the beginning. God made it clear that He was giving man authority over His creation, and that He wanted to fill the earth with those bearing His image! Now, let that sink into your mind. God gave man the command to have dominion over His creation, and He commanded man to fill the earth with those made in *His* image. This is the first time the Bible gives us a look at God's strategy of *Missions* from the very beginning of human history.

Shortly thereafter, the woman was deceived by Satan and did the one thing that God forbid her and her husband to do – eat the fruit from the tree in the midst of the garden. Her husband, Adam, was not deceived into eating the fruit, in disobedience to God's command. His disobedience was willful, and through this direct transgression by its *Federal Head* the entire human race fell into sin and, in Adam, was separated from God. This was no surprise to the omniscient, omnipotent God. He already had a plan through which man could be restored to a right relationship with Him, and this is found in His thesis statement of Genesis 3:15. In this statement, God promised a *Son* who would execute His plan of reconciliation.

Despite the fact that, through sin, the image of God was now *marred,* God's dominion mandate was not rescinded. They were still to fill the earth with those made in the image of God. So, God mercifully expelled man from the Garden, and Adam and his wife immediately produced offspring in obedience to God's dominion mandate. Why do I say that Man was *mercifully expelled* from the Garden? Had he been allowed to stay; God knew that Man would eat of the Tree of Life and therefore live forever separated from God. Since the mandate to be fruitful and multiply was not rescinded, such reproduction of these (now marred) *image bearers* continued through the *generations of Adam* and included the Sons of Promise, previously discussed in chapter 2.

If only Noah had written a book – *The Secret to Finding God's Grace!*

In Genesis 6:5-8 we read, "Then the LORD saw that the wickedness of man was great on the earth, and that every intent of the thoughts of his heart was only evil continually. (This is an incredible change from when God pronounced everything, He created to be *very good* in Genesis 1:31!) The LORD was sorry that He had made man on the earth, and He was grieved in His heart. The LORD said, I will blot out man whom I have created from the face of the land, from man to animals to creeping things and to birds of the sky; for I am sorry that I have made them. But Noah found grace in the eyes of the LORD." This is the first mention of the word *grace* in scripture, though God had demonstrated grace before this when He spared the physical lives of Adam and Eve. Now, we're told almost nothing about Noah before he shows up in the story. Maybe that's why he's named *Noah,* because, when he shows up, we don't *know-a* thing about him! So, how did Noah find *grace* in the eyes of the LORD? We don't know. The Bible doesn't tell us. If only Noah had written a book – *The Secret to Finding God's Grace!* No, by definition, *grace* means that Noah did nothing, made no contribution, to receive God's *grace!* If you try to do anything to *earn* grace you destroy what it is. Romans 11:6 says, "But if it is by grace (Greek - *charis - unmerited favor*), it is no longer on the basis of works, otherwise grace is no longer grace." The Hebrew word for *grace* is *chen* (pronounced *fein*). It literally means *to stoop.* Therefore, *grace* is God, of His own volition and purpose, *stooping* to show unmerited favor to man. God showed *grace* to Noah by allowing him to be the one through whom God would preserve and advance His divine plan to provide the deliverer promised in Genesis 3:15.

Through the building and population of the ark, God graciously saved Noah and 7 members of his family (see Genesis 6:9, the *generations of Noah,* through 8:22). The ark is a "type" or "foreshadowing" of Christ. God brought the animals that He had chosen into the ark at His appointed time. In John 6:44 Jesus says, "no man can come to me unless the Father who sent me draws him; and I will raise him up at the last day." Noah and his family were divinely chosen and *separated* unto the ark. 2 Corinthians 6:17 says, "Wherefore, come out from among them, and be ye separate, saith the Lord..." Noah and his family were *sheltered* by the ark. Romans 8:1 says, "There is therefore now no condemnation to them which are in Christ Jesus, who walk not after the flesh, but after the Spirit." Noah and his family were *supplied* by the ark. Philippians 4:19 says, "And my God will supply all your need according to his riches in glory in Christ Jesus." Noah and his family were totally *secured* in the ark. In John 10:28-30 Jesus said, "I give eternal life to them, and they will never perish; and no one will snatch them out of My hand. My Father, who has given them to Me, is greater than all; and no one is able to snatch them out of the Father's hand. I and the Father are one." Noah could've fallen down 1000 times inside the ark, but he could not fall out! 1 Corinthians 15:22 says, "As *in-Adam* all die, so *in-Christ* shall all be made alive." A Christian may stumble in Christ 1000 times, but he cannot fall out! Everyone outside the ark was utterly destroyed, while everyone inside the ark was totally secured. Therefore, it is in Christ. At the judgement, everyone not in-Christ will be utterly destroyed, while everyone in-Christ will be totally secured and glorified! Author's note: For further study see GTY.org John MacArthur series on Origins.

God's Dominion Mandate Repeated

> **There is only *one Race, and that is the Human Race!*
> There are many *ethnicities,* but only *one Race!***

In Genesis 9:1 and 9:7 God repeats the Dominion Mandate that He had given to Adam and Eve at the beginning of human history. To Noah and the 7 other survivors of the worldwide flood God said, "As for you, be fruitful and multiply; Populate the earth abundantly and multiply in it." That is *Missions*. It remained God's plan to fill the earth with His *image bearers,* and to bring forth *the seed of the woman* in fulfillment of His promise to pave a path whereby man could be reconciled to Himself. So, beginning in Genesis 10:1 we read, "Now these are the records of the generations of Shem, Ham, and Japheth, the sons of Noah; and sons were born to them after the flood." All through chapter 10 we find the listing of the offspring of Noah's three sons, and where they settled, appear. Then in Genesis 10:32 we read, "These are the families of the sons of Noah, according to their genealogies, by their *nations;* and out of these the *nations* were separated on the earth after the flood" (emphasis mine). Please don't miss this. All *nations* of the earth came from the offspring of Noah's three sons, Ham, Shem, and Japheth. In case you missed it, I'll state it for you; It There is only *one Race, and that is the Human Race!* There are many *ethnicities,* but only *one Race!* is amazing to hear God's people, the Church, engage in rhetoric, discussions, hand-wringing, and anguishing over *Race Relations!* The Church should lead the way in correcting the unbiblical, contemporary, ultra-dividing, definition of *Race,* including the hogwash *Critical Race Theory!* Critical Race Theory, or CRT, divides people into *identity groups* –dividing people into either the *oppressor class* (typically White, heterosexual, male, Christian) versus *victim identity groups* (typically Black or other Minority, LGBTQ+, women, disabled, abuse victims, and religious minorities). The point at which a person belongs to more than one category in the *victim identity group* is known as *Intersectionality.* For example, a person could be a Black, Transgender, disabled, abused, Muslim, which would identify them with five points of *intersection* as a victim. You can easily see how this is diametrically opposed to the very words of God, the Bible! As previously stated above, CRT divides people into *identity groups*. This is diametrically opposed to God's focus of dealing with people as *individuals!*

Next, in Genesis 11:1-4 we read, "Now the whole earth used the same language and the same words. It came about as they journeyed east, that they found a plain in the land of Shinar and settled there. They said to one another, Come, let us make bricks and burn them thoroughly. And they used brick for stone, and they used tar for mortar. They said, Come let us build for ourselves a city, and a tower whose top will reach into heaven, and let us make for ourselves a name, otherwise we will be scattered abroad over the face of the whole earth." Notice we see the people had the same language and the same words; this is exactly what we would expect from the same *Race*.

Please notice that the people had determined, under the leadership of the Apostate, Nimrod, to disobey *God's Dominion Mandate*. God said, "Be fruitful and multiply and subdue the (whole) earth, and have dominion over it." The people came to the plain of Shinar and said, "Let *us* build for *ourselves* a city, and a tower whose top will reach heaven. Let *us* make for *ourselves* a name, otherwise *we* will be scattered abroad over the face of the *whole earth.*" Translation? *Let us make ourselves great or else we'll find ourselves doing what God said do by multiplying His image bearers and filling the whole earth with them!*

I cannot possibly recall the number of sermons, and sermon references, that I've heard about this passage in Genesis 11. It is equally difficult for me to recall the multiple *theories* I've heard in these sermons as to why God came down and confused the languages of the people and scattered them over the whole earth. I've heard more than one preacher say, "God was afraid that the people would actually pierce heaven, and all of His secrets would be lost. So, He had to confuse their language so they couldn't communicate and that would stop the building project." There's nothing to speculate about here; Just read the text! God confused their language so that they couldn't communicate and follow their own program, but would, instead, be forced to follow *His Dominion Mandate!* It's not that hard! Just read the text! God had given them a *mission*. From the beginning, through the *Dominion Mandate*, it was always God's plan to fill the earth with people made in His image! God's plan of *Missions* is not something that began with the New Testament; it is not something that began with the arrival of the Messiah on earth! *Missions* is not something that began on the Day of Pentecost, nor with Jesus giving the Great Commission! God has *always* been on *mission!*

God's Continuation of Missions in Genesis

In the previous chapter we learned that Shem was Noah's son who was the *Son of Promise*, as he was the ancestor of Terah, Abram's father. God continued His plan for *Missions* through Abram. We see God's continuation of Missions in Genesis 12:1-3 where God gave the Abrahamic Covenant. In this covenant God promised "in you *all* the families of the earth shall be blessed." That's *Missions!* The Abrahamic Covenant was not just about God blessing Israel. God didn't intend to only bless one line, one people, or one nation. God made it clear that His plan was to use Abraham, and his seed, to be a blessing to *all nations on the earth.* That is *Missions.* Gentiles were in God's plan from the beginning, contrary to the popular idea that if the Jews had accepted Jesus the Gentiles would've been left out! Gentiles were never an afterthought!!! Gentiles are in view here. This blessing to Abraham was to be a blessing not only *to* the Jewish people, but also *through* the Jewish people to the rest of the world. All of the nations of the earth, who are not Israel, are Gentiles! So, God's inclusion of the Gentiles in His Mission to bring salvation through the *Seed of the Woman* is not an afterthought. It is inherent in the Abrahamic Covenant!

The Exodus Plagues Were to Advance Missions

Let's move to Exodus 9:14-16. "For this time, I will send all My plagues on you and your servants and your people, so that you may know that there is no one like Me in all the earth. For if by now I had put forth My hand and struck you and your people with pestilence, you would then have been cut off from the earth. But, indeed, for this reason I have allowed you to remain, in order to show you My power and in order to proclaim My name through all the earth." Here God gives us the purpose of the plagues. The purpose of the plagues was not simply so God's people could leave Egypt and exist in peace and quiet by themselves in isolation. The plagues had a three-fold purpose. Do you realize that God could have started with plague number ten, and Pharaoh would have immediately released His people! Then, why the other nine? I'm glad you asked. God's people had been in Egypt for 430 years. They were not allowed to worship Him in the way He specified, and they were perpetually exposed to the paganism of their captors.

> ### The tenth plague was to get His people out of Egypt.

First, the tenth plague was to get His people out of Egypt. Secondly, the other nine plagues were to *get Egypt out of God's people!* Each of those nine plagues were respectively directed at one of the Egyptian gods! God brought His people out of Egypt, but very quickly, it was clear that remnants of Egypt remained in His people. Where do you think they got the idea of making a golden calf? Of all the idols they could have made, why the calf? The bull was one of the pagan gods worshipped in Egypt! He was initially known as Apis, and later Osiris. Apis is a *Bull* god worshipped in Egypt at the time of the Jew's captivity in that land. Apis was purported to be the protector of the deceased the link to the pharaoh. He supposedly served as an intermediary between humans and the divine. This is where the Israelites in the wilderness got the idea of making a golden calf! Accordingly, it was clear that, though God had brought His people out of Egypt His people still had Egypt in them! Therefore, the nine plagues were for the purpose of getting Egypt out of God's people.

The third purpose for the plagues is found in God's statement to Pharaoh, "" ... *in order to show you My power and in order to proclaim My name through all the earth.*" God's purpose with Israel, in Israel, and through Israel was to have His name proclaimed in all the earth. God intended that the message of Israel and Israel's God would go into all the earth. That's *Missions!*

Remember, we're doing a survey so that we can be apprised of the fact that God has always been on *mission* and He didn't introduce this idea in Matthew 28.

What was God's purpose in establishing Israel's place among the nations? Turn to Deuteronomy 28:9-10. "The LORD will establish you as a holy people to Himself, as He swore to you, if you keep the commandments of the LORD your God and walk in His ways. So, all the peoples of the earth will see that you are called by the name of the LORD, and be afraid of you." – All the peoples of the earth will see that you are called by My name! That's *Missions!*

141

Chapter 15 Missions in the Old Testament

Missions Taught Through the Priests

We've seen God on *mission* in the Pentateuch. Now, turn to 1 Samuel 17:46. This is a very familiar story to us as Christians. However, I seriously doubt that we have read this and been aware that it is evidence of God being on *mission*. The text says, "This day the LORD will deliver you up into my hands, and I will strike you down and remove your head from you. And I will give the dead bodies of the army of the Philistines this day to the birds of the sky and the wild beasts of the earth, that all the earth may know that there is a God in Israel." David was not interested in all the earth knowing that there was a fierce little guy in Israel who was bad! No! David told Goliath that he would kill him and the Philistines, and feed them to the birds and the animals so that *all the earth would know that there's a God in Israel*. That is *Missions!*

Let's look at Israel's worship. Turn to 1 Chronicles 16:31. This was the occasion when the Israelites, under King David, were returning the Ark of the Covenant to Jerusalem. Here we read, "Let the heavens be glad, and let the earth rejoice; and let them say among the nations, the LORD reigns." – Let them say among the *nations* (Gentiles) the Lord reigns. That is *Missions!*

Next, let's give 'eye-gate' to 2 Chronicles 6:32-33. This is part of Solomon's prayer at the event of the dedication of the temple. "Also concerning the foreigner who is not from Your people Israel, when he comes from a far country for Your great name's sake and Your mighty hand and Your outstretched arm, when they come and pray toward this house, then hear from heaven, from Your dwelling place and do according to all for which the foreigner calls to You, in order that all the peoples of the earth may know Your name, and fear You as do Your people Israel, and that they may know that this house which I have built is called by Your name." Here we see the understanding that this temple is not just about Israel. This temple is a witness to the nations. That's *Missions!*

This verse has nothing to do with America! America has never been *God's people!*

---

2 Chronicles 7:14 is a very familiar verse. Notice that it follows 2 Chronicles 6:32-33, and is part of the same temple dedication. I'm sure that you can't count the number of times that you've probably heard this verse wrongly quoted and taken totally out of context! It reads, "If My people, which are called by My name, shall humble themselves, and pray, and seek My face, and turn from their wicked ways; then will I hear from heaven, and will forgive their sin, and will heal their land." It is simply amazing what violence has been done to this verse! So very many American Christians have perpetually quoted it to their friends, Pastors have forcefully proclaimed it to their parishioners, Televangelists have pounded the podium before audiences of hundreds of thousands, and they have applied this verse to America! They act as if the United States of America is a *Christendom- Christ's Kingdom.* Nothing is further from the truth! This verse has nothing to do with America! America has never been *God's people!* In context, Solomon is praying for the nation Israel. Compare what America approves and teaches with what the Bible commands, approves and teaches; it is as if America is trying to see just how fast and far, she can get away from being in step with anything that God commands, approves, and teaches! When we stand and with fervor and conviction sing "God bless America", nobody wants to acknowledge the elephant in the room; that is, why should God bless America? We pass laws to sanction and approve everything that is against His word – even the things that He clearly calls *abominations!* 2 Chronicles 7:14 applies, in context, to the nation of Israel, and only Israel! It is clear that in dedication of the temple using this verse, missions were high profile.

Missions in Poetic Literature of the O.T.

Let us now turn our survey to the Messianic Psalms. First, turn to Psalm 2:7-8. "I will surely tell of the decree of the LORD; He said to Me, You are My Son, today I have begotten You. Ask of Me, and I will surely give the nations as Your inheritance, and the very ends of the earth as Your possession. You shall break them with a rod of iron, You shall shatter them like earthenware. Now Therefore, O kings, show discernment; Take warning, O kings of the earth. Worship the LORD with reverence and rejoice with trembling. Do homage to the Son, that He not become angry, and you perish in the way, for His wrath may soon be kindled. How blessed are all who take refuge in Him!" That is *Missions!*

Now let us continue our survey to the poetic literature of the Psalms. Turn to Psalm 22:27-28. "All the ends of the earth will remember and turn to the LORD, and all the families of the nations will worship before You. For the kingdom is the LORD'S and He rules over the nations." Even as Israel sang their songs, (though they paid no conscious mind to it) they were reminding each other that God's plan included the nations.

Turn your Bibles to Psalm 46:10, where we read, "Be still and know that I am God. (Don't stop. At the end of your being still) I will be exalted among the nations. I will be exalted in all the earth." Now, be honest. How many times have you quoted the first half of that verse and given no thought to the second half? How many times have you heard other Christians do that? The second half is God's view of *Missions!*

Turn to Psalm 72:8-9. "May He have dominion from sea to sea, and from the river to the ends of the earth. May desert tribes bow down before Him, and His enemies lick the dust." This is missions!

Psalm 72:17-20 says, "May His name endure forever; May His name increase as long as the sun shines; and let men bless themselves by Him; Let all nations call him blessed. Blessed be the LORD God, the God of Israel, Who alone works wonders. And blessed be His glorious name forever; and may the whole earth be filled with His glory, Amen, and Amen." This is missions! In the Psalms we cannot miss this worldwide picture of *Missions*.

The Jewish Prophets Prophesied about Missions

We've seen God on mission in the Pentateuch, from the Priests, in the Poetic literature of the Psalms, and now let us survey the Prophets to see if we might find *Missions* there.

> **Gentiles were never an afterthought in the mind and heart of God. That's missions**

Isaiah 2:3 says, "And many peoples shall come and say, come let us go up to the mountain of the LORD, to the house of the God of Jacob; That He may teach us concerning His ways and that we may walk in His paths." We typically miss the *missions* emphasis in the word *peoples*. This is biblical language for *people groups*. This is clearly *not* talking only about Israel! The Gentiles were never an afterthought in the mind and heart of God. That's missions!

Isaiah 24:16 reads, "From the ends of the earth we hear songs, Glory to the Righteous One, but I say woe to me! Woe to me! Alas for me!" This is in the section of Isaiah's prophesy that details God's judgement on His chosen nation, Israel. This is the Prophet predicting that Gentiles will be praising and glorifying God while all hell is breaking loose in the nation of Israel and for her people! That is missions!

In Jeremiah 3:17 we read, "At that time they will call Jerusalem the Throne of the LORD, and all the nations will be gathered to it, to Jerusalem, for the name of the LORD; Nor will they walk anymore after the stubbornness of their evil heart." Here is the Prophet predicting the salvation of Gentiles. That speaks of God's *Missions* mindset!

Jeremiah 16:19 says, "O LORD, my strength and my stronghold, and my refuge in the day of distress, to You the nations will come from the ends of the earth and say, our fathers have inherited nothing but falsehood, futility and things of no profit. Can man make Gods for himself? Yet they are not Gods! Therefore, behold, I am going to make them know this time I will make them know My power and My might; and they shall know that My name is the LORD." In the scriptures, when you see the word *nations, peoples, or Gentiles,* God is talking about everyone *except* Israel. When you see *The Nation* (singular) God is excluding everyone *except* Israel. Once again, we see God's missional heart toward the Gentiles.

Micah 5:2-4, says, "But as for you, Bethlehem Ephrata, too little to be among the clans of Judah, from you One will go forth for Me to be ruler in Israel. His goings forth are from long ago, from the days of eternity. Therefore, He will give them up until the time when she who is in labor has borne a child, then the remainder of His brethren will return to the sons of Israel, and He will arise and shepherd His flock in the strength of the LORD, in the majesty of the name of the LORD His God. And they will remain because at that time He will be great to the ends of the earth." This is specifically about the Lord Jesus Christ, and here God's mission mindset is in full view!

Zechariah 2:11 says, "Many nations will join themselves to the LORD in that day and will become My people." Here the Prophet is prophesying concerning the captivity of Israel in Babylon. This is prior to the time when Israel, as a nation, will turn to Jesus Christ and will look back and lament over how they rejected the Messiah (Isaiah 52:13 through chapter 53). In the midst of this, the Prophet prophesies that many nations will join themselves to the LORD. The Father drawing these nations to Christ is Missions! I remind you that in John 6:44 Jesus said, "No man can come to Me except the Father who sent me draws him."

Look to Habakkuk 2:14. "For the earth shall be filled with the knowledge of the glory of the LORD, as the waters cover the sea." This is the Prophet's predicting the outcome of *Missions.*

The Israelites are God's chosen people, through whom He chose to bring the *Son of Promise,* the Lord Jesus Christ, to be the *Deliverer* who would produce the Spiritual descendants of Abraham. It was obvious that there would be Jewish Spiritual descendants of Abraham. However, we usually miss the prevalent prophecy concerning *Gentile* Abrahamic descendants all through the Old Testament. That is *missions.* The New Testament confirms this. Ephesians 2:13-16 tells us that God made the two, Jew and Gentile, into one people. "But now in Christ Jesus you who formerly were far off have been brought near by the blood of Christ. For He Himself is our peace who made both groups into one and broke down the barrier of the dividing wall, by abolishing in His flesh the enmity, which is the Law of commandments contained in ordinances, so that in Himself He might make the two into one new man, thus establishing peace, and might reconcile them both in one body to God through the cross, by it having put to death the enmity." God does not have two distinct, separate peoples. Replacement Theology is absurd! God has not changed His mind! It has always been His plan that His children would include, both, Jew and Gentile.

By faith, I am a descendant of Abraham. Galatians 3:6-9 says, "Even so Abraham believed God and it was reckoned to him as righteousness. Therefore, be sure that it is those who are of faith who are the sons of Abraham. The scripture, foreseeing that God would justify the Gentiles by faith, preached the gospel beforehand to Abraham saying, all the nations will be blessed in you. So, then those who are of faith are blessed with Abraham the believer." Paul pulled this from Genesis 12:3. This is the realization of what we find throughout the Old Testament; God has always been on mission to, not only save Jews, but also Gentiles!

Malachi 1:11 – "My name will be great among the nations..." Could this statement possibly be any clearer that missions among the Gentiles have always been part of God's plan?

From the beginning to the end of the Old Testament God has always displayed His Missions mindset. Matthew 28, The Great Commission, is not a new idea. From the beginning, God has had and advanced a *Missions* agenda. This is why the Jewish Apostles were so excited about seeing Gentiles come to faith, because this was the fulfillment of God's promise to His people Israel.

Thousands of years ago, Jewish people sang songs crying out to God believing, hoping, and praying that God would bring this (Gentiles coming to Him) to fruition.

Chronologically, *missions* began in the book of Genesis. However, *missions* in the heart and mind of God, Father, Son, and Holy Spirit, started before the world began! Next, we will turn out attention to missions in the New Testament.

Chapter 16 Missions In the Gospels and the Book of Acts

> ## The Lord's Prayer in John 17. Luke 11 and Matthew 6:9-13 are *not* the Lord's Prayer.

In order to truly see how Missions began in eternity past, before the Old Testament was written, we must survey The Lord's Prayer in John 17. Luke 11 and Matthew 6:9-13 are *not* the Lord's Prayer. They represent the *Model or Pattern Prayer.* Therefore, the *Lord's Prayer* is in John 17 where the Lord Jesus is in prayer throughout the entire chapter.

To see that Missions began in eternity past is very important, because many of us have a man-centered view of salvation; that is the view that salvation starts with us as it's reason. We tend to think of God as some benevolent super hero, who saw our impending doom and sprang into action to save us out of His pity. Others think God took action to save us because, somehow, He needed us. Neither of these scenarios is even in the hemisphere of truth! Factually, Biblically, the doctrine of the *Covenant of Redemption* starts in eternity past in the Godhead, *not* with you and me.

This actually begins our survey of Missions in the New Testament. First, let us consider some of the narrative phrases of John 17. verse 1, "Father, the hour has come; glorify your Son that the Son may glorify you." Verse 5, "now, Father, glorify me in your own presence with the glory that I had with you before the world existed." Skip down to verse 23, "I in them and you in me, that they may become perfectly one, *so that the world may know* that you sent me and loved them even as you loved me. Father, I desire that they also, whom you have given me, may be with me where I am, to see my glory that you have given me because you loved me before the foundation of the world." The Covenant of Redemption is established in eternity within the Godhead. It's established before the world began. This is important, because it was part of God's design since before the world began that we would belong to Him! You, Christian, are not an afterthought. You are here, by the grace of God, for His purpose! The Covenant of Redemption is rooted and grounded in eternity past.

The Covenant of Redemption begins with the love of God within the Godhead. Look again at verses 23-24, "I in them and you in me, that they may become perfectly one, so that the world may know that *you sent me and loved them even as you loved me.* Father, I desire that they also, whom you have given me, may be with me where I am, to see my glory that you have given me because you loved me before the foundation of the world." Now look at verse 26. "And I have made Your name known to them, and will make it known, *so that the love with which You loved Me may be in them, and I in them.*" The Covenant of Redemption is important not only because it begins in eternity past but because it's rooted in the love of the Godhead. It's not rooted in imperfect horizontal love, (human to human). It is rooted in perfect vertical love (God to man first, then man to God). One of the reasons that Christians espouse the ridiculous notion that salvation can be lost is because they don't understand that it is based on this vertical love!

These Christians have camped on one of the horizontal metaphors and it doesn't allow that the root of our salvation is found in vertical love. Maybe their whole salvation paradigm is based on the *marriage* metaphor, or *the family and adoption* metaphor. So, they look at their marriage, or their parents' marriage and see that marriages sometimes fail. Therefore, by that metaphor, salvation can be lost! How many people have I counseled with over the years, who says they have a hard time embracing the love of Father God because they had such a terrible human father? Even Martin Luther fell victim to this for the first 25 years of his Christian life, because he had a horrible human father!

Maybe you come from a family that has no sense of *forgiveness,* and suddenly, by the grace of God, you find yourself in a new family because He has forgiven you. However, your only understanding of what forgiveness means comes from your unforgiving, spiteful, vindictive human family. How, in the name of heaven, can you totally, comfortably, rest in the forgiveness of God?

You see, when we start *horizontally,* we have a problem but God's love for his people does *not* begin *horizontally,* it begins *vertically.* It's rooted and grounded in the love of the Godhead, in the love that the Father has for his Son, the perfect love that has existed in the Godhead throughout all eternity that has never failed and that can never fail. When we see imperfect examples what we have to realize is this: you don't go from the imperfect to the perfect, you go from the perfect to the imperfect. I don't look at my imperfect father or my children don't look at their imperfect father and say, "Well, that's what fatherhood is, therefore God is imperfect." No, we start with the perfect Father, God, and we say, "That's what fatherhood is and this is why I can never be satisfied with an imperfect human father. It's alright, because there is a perfect Father." We do not start with the imperfect love that humans have for each other; we start with the perfect love that the Father has for the Son. This perfect love is personified in the person of the Holy Spirit. You do not start with the horizontal and the imperfect; you start with the vertical and the perfect.

The Covenant of Redemption is rooted and grounded in eternity. It's rooted and grounded in the Trinity. It is rooted and grounded in a love gift that the Father gave to his Son. This is the heart of the doctrine of salvation.

Look at this. This is a common problem. If we start with the horizontal love paradigm, we take a *democratic* view of salvation. A *democratic* view of salvation says that salvation is up to the individual; it's what the individual thinks about it. *God is not running for God!* There is one God and no runners up! He's not after your approval. He's God. Therefore, instead of taking this horizontal picture and imposing it upon God, we must look at what God says about himself!

Look at John 17 verses 1 and 2 together. "When Jesus had spoken these words, he lifted up his eyes to heaven, and said, 'Father, the hour has come; glorify your Son that the Son may glorify you, since you have given him authority over all flesh, to give eternal life to *all whom you have given him."* Skip down to verse 6, "I have manifested your name to the people *whom you gave me* out of the world. Yours they were, and *you gave them to me*, and they have kept your word." Look at Verse 9, "I am praying for them. I am not praying for the world but for *those whom you have given me, for they are yours*." Look at verse 11. "I am no longer in the world; and yet they themselves are in the world, and I come to You. Holy Father, keep them in Your name, the name *which you gave given Me*, that they may be one even as We are." Verse 12, "While I was with them, I was keeping them in Your name *which You have given Me*; and I guarded them and not one of them perished but the son of perdition, so that the scripture would be fulfilled." Now verse 24 reads, "Father, I desire that they also, *whom you have given me*, may be with me where I am." *Whom you have given me.*

In eternity past, the Father gave a gift to the Son, and that gift that he gave was a people for His possession because of his love for the Son. God's saving grace on you does not begin with His love for you; it begins with the Father's love for the Son! The Father has loved the Son for all eternity and will never stop loving the Son, which means that if my salvation is rooted and grounded in the

Father's love for the Son, it is as secure as the Trinity! The Son, because of His love for his Father, gave His life in order to redeem those whom the Father had given to Him before the world began. Then, the Holy Spirit, who is the personification of the love between the Father and the Son, applies the redemption that the Son achieved, in time, to all those for whom the Son died. It starts at eternity past; it's rooted and grounded in the love that the Father has for the Son and in a love gift that the Father gave to the Son.

> **Your salvation begins and ends with God! Can you lose your salvation? Only if God can stop being God.**

Your salvation begins and ends with God! Can you lose your salvation? Only if God can stop being God. That is what would need to happen for one who is redeemed, by the Lord Jesus Christ, to lose his/her salvation. The Trinity would have to cease to exist in order for that to happen! You see, this is all about the glory of God! John 17 tells us this repeatedly!

There's more about Missions in the New Testament than just the Great Commission.

Turn your Bible to Matthew 10:16 -18. "Behold, I send you out as sheep in the midst of wolves; so be shrewd as serpents and innocent as doves. But beware of men, for they will hand you over to the courts and scourge you in their synagogues; and you will even be brought before governors and kings for My sake, *as a testimony to them and to the Gentiles*." Jesus said that being sent to re-pre-sent Him, and even the potential scourgings, were all about *missions* to the Gentiles!

Turn your Bible to Matthew 24:14. We know that this chapter is about eschatology – the end times – just prior to Jesus' second coming. It says, "This gospel of the kingdom shall be preached in the whole world as a testimony to all the nations, and then the end will come." That is Missions! Unfortunately, most Christians are enthused and wrapped around knowing when the end will come instead of being engaged in of making disciples of all nations, which will facilitate the end! Such is our dismissal and shortsightedness concerning Missions!

Of course, we have the famous Missions verses found in Matthew 28:18-20. "All authority is given to Me in heaven and in earth. Therefore, go and make disciples of all nations, baptizing them in the name of the Father, and in the name of the Son, and in the name of the Holy Ghost, and teaching them to obey all that I have commanded you. And lo, I am with you always, even unto the end of the age." We'll deal with this extensively later.

Now turn to Mark 11:15-17. This very familiar passage recounts one of the two occurrences of Jesus clearing out the temple. It reads, "Then they came to Jerusalem. And He entered the temple and began to drive out those who were buying and selling in the temple, and overturned the tables of the money changers and the seats of those who were selling doves; and He would not permit anyone to carry merchandise through the temple. And He began to teach and say to them, is it not written, My house shall be called a house of prayer *for all the nations?* But you have made it a robber's den." Now, be honest. When you quote verse 17, or hear it quoted, usually, is not the last part of the verse left out? Yeah…that would be the part that says, "for all the nations." That is the part about Missions!

Look at Mark 16:14-15. This is Mark's statement of the Great Commission. "Afterward He appeared to the eleven themselves as they were reclining at the table; and He reproached them for their unbelief and hardness of heart, because they had not believed those who had seen Him after He had risen. And He said to them, Go, into all the world and preach the gospel to all creation." That is Missions!

Look at the *Model Prayer* in Luke 11:1,2. This is *not* the Lord's Prayer, as taught by tradition. It is the *Pattern or Model Prayer.* Why is it impossible for this to be the *Lord's Prayer?* The first reason this can not be the *Lord's Prayer* is found in Verse 1. This verse tells us that Jesus was praying, and when He finished, His disciples said, "Lord, teach us to pray just as John (the Baptist) taught his disciples. Jesus opened His mouth and said unto them, when *you pray* say..." The second reason that this cannot be the *Lord's Prayer* is found in verse 4, which says, "...and forgive us our sins as we forgive those who sin against us." Jesus had no sin! Therefore, He could never validly pray this prayer for Himself! The Lord's Prayer is found in John 17 where Jesus is in prayer throughout the whole chapter! Do you see what tradition has done to us?

In the Model prayer, of Luke 11, the first three petitions center on the glory of God – specifically the glory of God among men on earth. "Hallowed be Thy name, thy kingdom come, they will be done, as in heaven so in earth." This part of the prayer asked God to make His name to be honored, that His kingdom shall be believed by us and all men, and that all men on earth serve God as the angels do in heaven. That is a *missional* prayer!

Turn in your Bibles to Luke 2:29-32. This is the prophecy of Simeon at the circumcision of the baby Jesus, when He was eight days old. "Now Lord, you are releasing Your bond-servant to depart in peace, according to Your word; For my eyes have seen Your salvation, which You have prepared in the presence of all peoples, a light of revelation to the Gentiles, and the glory of Your people Israel." The phrase "a light of revelation to the Gentiles" is clearly Missions!

Turn your Bible to Luke 10:1-2. This is the event of Jesus sending out the seventy to preach the gospel. It reads, "Now after this the Lord appointed seventy others, and sent them in pairs ahead of Him to every city and place where He Himself was going to come. And He was saying to them, the harvest is plentiful, but the laborers are few; therefore, beseech the Lord of the harvest to send out laborers into His harvest." The ones that He commanded to pray that the Lord of the harvest would send out laborers were the ones being immediately sent! That is Missions!

Turn your Bible to John 12:31-32. "Now judgment is upon this world; now the ruler of this world will be cast out. And I, if I am lifted up from the earth, will draw all men to Myself." We Christians sing a song based on verse 32. The lyrics say, "If I, if I be lifted up from the earth, I'll draw all men unto Me." *Lifted up*, in that song, is interpreted as being *lifted up in praise*. The only thing wrong with it is that it is wrong! In Jesus' day, that term meant to be *lifted up on a cross – to be crucified!* The part I don't want you to miss is the last sentence in verse 32. We usually pay no attention to verse 33, which says, "But He was saying this to indicate the kind of death by which He was to die." Jesus is saying, that if/when He is crucified that He will draw all men unto Himself. That is Missions!

Please understand this; *narrative is not normative!*

Now, leave the gospels and go to the book of Acts – specifically Acts 1:8. This is the thesis statement for the book of Acts. I've heard many Christian Pastors say, "We need to go back and be like the church in the book of Acts. That's all we need to do!" If all we needed was to be like the church in Acts, why did God give us the Epistles? It was never God's intention for us to be identical to the church in the book of Acts. Most say this out of a bias for suggesting that the *sign gifts* exercised in the book of Acts are to be exercised by the church today. *Nothing is further from the truth!* The book of

Acts is a historical narrative of how the early church advanced in fulfilling the Great Commission. Please understand this; *narrative is not normative!* Everything that happened in the Book of Acts is *not* to be reproduced in and through the church of today. All one need do is study the narrative about Ananias and Saphira, and then thank almighty God that *narrative is not normative!* Acts 1:8 says, "You shall be witnesses unto Me both, in Jerusalem, and in all Judea, and in Samaria, and to the uttermost parts of the earth." What that says is that your (individual Christian) sphere of influence for Christ will simultaneously be in those four areas. Your local situation – Jerusalem. Your neighboring situation – Judea. The people of your worst prejudice – Samaria (that's who the Samaritans represented to the people to whom Jesus was giving this command). Then, to the last fragment of humanity – the ends of the earth. That's Missions! Oh, by the way…When Jesus spoke this command to those men, where He spoke it, WE, in the Western Hemisphere, were at the ends of the earth! Aren't you glad they obeyed His command?

Now, turn your Bible to Acts 13:46-49. This is the message of Paul and Barnabas to the Jews at Antioch. "Paul and Barnabas spoke out boldly and said, It was necessary that the word of God be spoken to you first; since you repudiate it and judge yourselves unworthy of eternal life, behold, we are turning to the Gentiles; For so the Lord has commanded us, I have placed you as a light for the Gentiles, that you may bring salvation to the end of the earth. When the Gentiles heard this, they began rejoicing and glorifying the word of the Lord; and as many as had been appointed (this is the electing grace of God in your salvation) to eternal life believed. And the word of the Lord was being spread through the whole region." No commentary is required here! This is Missions!

Missions in the Epistles & Revelation

We've seen Missions in the Gospels and the Book of Acts. Now let's look at Missions in the epistles.

Turn to Romans 1:1-5. It reads, "Paul, a bond-servant of Christ Jesus, called as an apostle, set apart for the gospel of God, which He promised beforehand through His prophets in the holy scriptures, concerning His Son, who was born of a descendant of David according to the flesh, who was declared the Son of God with power by the resurrection from the dead, according to the Spirit of holiness, Jesus Christ our Lord, through whom we have received grace and apostleship *to bring about the obedience of faith among all the Gentiles for His name's sake."* This is Missions!

Romans 10:12-15 says, "For there is no distinction between Jew and Greek; for the same Lord is Lord of all, abounding in riches for all who call on Him; for whoever will call on the name of the Lord will be saved. How then will they call on Him in whom they have not believed? How will they believe in Him whom they have not heard? And how will they hear without a preacher? How will they preach unless they are sent? Just as it is written, How beautiful are the feet of those who bring good news of good things!" This is Missions!

Galatians 3:8 tells us, "The scripture, foreseeing that God would justify the Gentiles by faith, preached the gospel beforehand to Abraham, saying All the nations will be blessed in you. So then those who are of faith are blessed with Abraham the believer." That is Missions!

In Revelation 5:9-10 we read, "And they sang a new song, saying, worthy are You to take the book and to break its seals; for You were slain, and purchased for God with Your blood men from every tribe and tongue and people and nation. You have made them to be a kingdom and priests to our God; and they will reign upon the earth." That is the result of Missions!

In Revelation 7:9-11 we read, "After these things I looked, and behold, a great multitude which no one could count, from every nation and all tribes and peoples and tongues, standing before the throne and before the Lamb, clothed in white robes, and palm branches were in their hands; and they cry out with a loud voice saying, Salvation to our God who sits on the throne, and to the Lamb." That is the crowning result of Missions!

Chapter 17 Christ's Primary Mission Statement
Matthew 28:16-20

The last words of any person are considered important, and are honored, and never forgotten by those who truly love that person. Further, the more important the person, the more important the last words. If these last words take the form of a request or a command to the people that truly love that person, they will honor them at great costs and tremendous risks.

Did you happen to see the made for TV series called "Lonesome Dove?" If so, you will remember the scene where one of the heroes of the story, Gus, (Robert Duvall) was wounded and hovering near death. He called his lifetime best friend, the Colonel, (Tommy Lee Jones) to his bed and gave him the charge to take his body, after death, on a long perilous journey across the Wild West, back to Texas. He gave the Colonel explicit instructions as to where to bury him once he got the body back to Texas. After his death, the Colonel set out to honor his friend's last words. He faced many, many dangers along the way. He survived Indian attack, crossed raging flooded streams, staved off wild animals, and survived ambush by bandits. Nevertheless, through it all, he was undeterred. He was determined, *with every fiber of his being,* to carry out the final command of his friend, and did. Why did the Colonel do this? Was it simply because it was his friend's last wish? No! It was because of the love he had for his friend that he was obedient (at all costs) to his friend's final command.

As you hear this message, realize these are the last words of the Lord to His followers before He ascended back to heaven. We sit in our assemblies and sing "Oh, how I love Jesus"! Ask yourself, honestly before God, if you're honoring the final instructions of our

LORD *with every fiber of your being, which proves that love that you sing about!*

> **Matthew's genealogy establishes that, had there been a King on the throne of Israel during this period, Joseph (Jesus' adoptive Father) would've been the rightful ruler.**

We finally come to the epic center of God's focus on *Missions*. If one studies through Matthew and misses the meaning of this text one has missed the purpose of Matthew's gospel, and God's thesis statement in Genesis 3:15. This is not the end of Matthew's gospel, but rather, it is the climax of his gospel account! This is where God has been headed since giving us His thesis statement pointing *to the seed of the woman.* This is where Matthew has been going from the time, he introduced the genealogy of Jesus back in chapter one. Matthew's gospel highlights Jesus as the King, both, heavenly and Israel's earthly King. Matthew's genealogy establishes that, had there been a King on the throne of Israel during this period, Joseph (Jesus' adoptive Father) would've been the rightful ruler. When Joseph died, his legal heir, Jesus, would have been the heir to that earthly throne, and would have been the earthly King of Israel! In our text, at the climax of Matthew's gospel account, he highlights that Jesus, having all authority in heaven and earth, is the King of heaven and of the entire universe!

Just as this text represents the climax of Matthew's gospel, it also represents the climax of Jesus' physical time on earth! From eternity past through His conception, He has been progressing, in God's timing, on God's schedule, toward this climax! Therefore, it is here that He stands on a mountain in Galilee in the only prescheduled post-resurrection meeting with His Disciples to charge them, and all future generations of believers, with His final orders of operation. Take your Bible and turn to Matthew 28:16-20, and we will carefully examine His final instructions to the people who loved Him most. These are also HIS final instructions to US HIS followers. Bear this in mind.

"But the eleven disciples proceeded to Galilee, to the mountain which Jesus had designated. When they saw Him. They worshipped Him, but some were doubtful. And Jesus came up and spoke to them, saying, all authority has been given to Me in heaven and on earth. Go therefore, and make disciples of all the nations, baptizing them in the name of the Father, and the Son, and the Holy Spirit, teaching them to observe all that I have commanded you: and lo, I am with you always even unto the end of the age."

This statement that we have just read has rightly been called "The Great Commission." It is the mighty mandate of our Lord to us His children. It is a command to each and every person who claims to be a follower of the Lord Jesus Christ. There are no exceptions, no exclusions, no exemptions, nobody is left out! What is truly amazing is how little most followers of Christ know and understand about these marching orders.

I'm reminded of the story of what happened in a missions' conference that took place several years ago in the Upper Peninsula of Michigan. At the beginning of a Disciple Making Conference for pastors and church leaders, the question was asked, "What is the Great Commission?" The instructions were to write their answer down on a piece of paper and hand it in. One Pastor, who had apparently never heard the term, wrote, *"The Great Commission is the personal profit of a real estate agent on an unusually large property sale."* This was the answer of a man who had been cut out of the flock of God to lead His flock, and the man was unaware of Jesus' final instructions to His followers!

Many of you work for corporations, or businesses. If you went to the corporate website, you would find there, a *mission statement*. That mission statement would articulate for what purpose that business exists. Every good business makes certain that all of its employees know what the mission statement of that organization is. The Great Commission is God's *mission statement* given by the One Who fulfilled the prophecy in God's *thesis statement* in Genesis 3:15. Here stands the prophesied *seed of the woman* who has had His *heel bruised* at Golgotha on the cross, and there *crushed* the serpent's (Satan's) head in defeat! Hebrews 2:14 & 15 states it like this, "Therefore, since the children share in flesh and blood, He Himself likewise also partook of the same, that through death He might render powerless him who had the power of death, that is the devil, and might free those who through fear of death were subject to slavery all their lives." Because of what He has accomplished, here stands *the Son of Promise, David's greater Son,* the Lord Jesus Christ, declaring that "all authority in heaven and earth" (anywhere and everywhere) has been given to Him. Therefore, He *commands* the continuation of the pursuit of God's mission by each and every one of His followers!

What is God's mission, and how is it to be accomplished? Listen to Jesus. John 6:38 says, "For I have come down from heaven, not to do My own will, but the will of Him who sent Me." What is the Father's will? Again, listen to Jesus, in Luke 19:10 where we read, "For the Son of Man has come to seek and to save that which was lost." How did Jesus accomplish this salvation? In John 19:30, the scripture says, "Therefore when Jesus had received the sour wine, He said it is finished, and He bowed His head and gave up His spirit." This portion of John's gospel provides the details of Christ's crucifixion. This is the fulfillment of Genesis 3:15, God's thesis statement. This is how *the seed of the woman* accomplished the Father's will of seeking and saving the lost through *Redemption.*

However, *Redemption* was not enough! Now, inevitably, someone will jump quickly to their feet and scream *"Blasphemy!"* Relax for a moment, drop the stones, and turn your Bible to John 17:4. There will still be plenty of time for stoning me after this, if you're still of the mind to do so! In the *Lord's Prayer* of John 17:4 Jesus says in prayer to the Father, "I have glorified You on the earth, *having accomplished* (past tense in English and Greek) the work which You have given Me to do." Now, what work was Jesus referring to here? You can consult commentary after commentary, and they will continually tell you that Jesus is here talking about the work of *Redemption*. That *cannot* be accurate, because the cross of *Redemption* is still two chapters away in John 19! No! Here Jesus is talking about the work of *Reproduction through Disciple Making!* Need more evidence? Do not rush for the stones just yet! The *Lord's Prayer* outlines like this: In verses 1-5, He prays for Himself. In verse 6-19 He prays for His immediate 11 Disciples (Judas is gone to do the deed). In verses 20 and following, He prays for all future generations of Disciples, and that is where you and I get in on the petition (if we're following His plan) as if He called our very names! On His way to the cross, in our Lord's *High Priestly Prayer,* in just over 23 verses He prays for *Disciples* 46 times!!! Therefore, in accomplishing the Father's will, Jesus came to do *two things!* Had He only accomplished *Redemption and not Reproduction,* Christianity would have died in the first generation. Had He only accomplished *Reproduction and not Redemption,* there would have been no good news to tell. Therefore, Jesus, necessarily, came to do *two* things: *Reproduction* through His strategy of Disciple Making, and *Redemption* through His work on the cross! He has given us the pursuit of that same mission through *ordinary means.* We are to offer men *Redemption* through the proclamation of the gospel of Jesus Christ; the Father will draw men and women through the gospel message. Paul declares in Romans 1:16, "For I am not ashamed of the gospel of Jesus Christ for IT (emphasis mine) is the power of God unto salvation; to the Jew first and then to the Greek." God uses the power of the gospel to draw men and women to Christ. John 6:44 says, "No one can come to Me unless the Father who sent Me draws him; and I will raise him up on the last day." Then, Jesus *commands* us to turn those, whom the Father draws, into the same thing Jesus turned the 12 into…Disciples through the ordinary means of making Disciples!

Notice that I intentionally emphasized that every follower of Jesus Christ is *commanded* to make Disciples.

This is NOT just the mission statement of Pastors and Missionaries!

Our LORD'S Great Commission is the *mission statement* of all/each of His followers. The *Church* is made up of the collection of all followers of Jesus Christ. 1 Corinthians 3:16 says, "You are the temple of God…" There are two Greek words that translate by our English word *Temple*. One is *hieron;* this word describes the Temple *precinct*. The Temple complex stretched over a 32-acre space in Jesus' day. That would be *hieron*. The second Greek word translated by our English word *Temple* is *Naos*. This is the word for the *holy of holies,* and is the word used here. This is the word describing the place where the presence of God dwelt. So, Paul is saying, "What in the world is wrong with you Christians? Do you not know that you are the place where the very presence of God dwells? You are the holiest place on earth! You're the *Temple* of almighty God!" What's a temple for? To contain a God! For what purpose does the temple exist? To show off the God Who is contained and worshipped there in the community where that Temple happens to be located!

The Church is *not* the building, or the institution. The Church is made up of each individual follower who was, personally, given this Great Commission by our Lord! It follows, then, that this is what the church is to be all about. Do not confuse my reference to "the

165

church" to mean the *institution.* YOU – Believer(s) – are the temple of God! YOU constitute the *church!* Obedience to the command to Make Disciples was given to you, individually! This is what we are to do. This is what *I* am to do. This is what *You* are to do. The building where the church meets is to be the *base of* ministry, and not the *place for* ministry!

Are We following the *Savior's Strategy,* or *Satan's Subtle Substitute?*

This is the *Savior's Strategy!* By command, He addresses each and every one of His followers, individually, with the Great Commission. What is *Satan's Subtle Substitute* at this point? He, through the Roman Emperor, Constantine, shifted the common meaning of *church* from what you, the believers, are to describe the place where believers meet! Why is this subtle change in definition critical? What you *go to* you can leave, but what you *are* you *are* all of the time! More on this in a moment.

So, this is the mission statement of every individual follower of the Lord Jesus Christ! This not just the mission statement of Missionaries, Pastors, Elders, and Deacons. This is the mission statement of anyone who claims to be a follower of Jesus Christ! If you take this, the final command of the Lord Jesus Christ, seriously, it will radically affect everything you do and every plan you make.

Late in life, the great writer, Rudyard Kipling, said, "For years now I have never left home without my Six Editorial Friends; They are, Who, What, Where, When, How, and Why." If a reporter from the local newspaper was dispatched to cover a story, and that reporter failed to answer one of those six editorial questions, then that reporter has violated the story, and the *truth* has not been reported. Our text, in the next chapter, beautifully answers these Six Editorial Questions!

Chapter 18 The Six Editorial Friends of the Great Commission

In this statement, we are told *Who* is to obey the Command in the Commission. We are told *What* to do in obeying the Command in the Commission. We are told *Where* to perform this in obedience to the Command in the Commission. We are told *When* we are to obey the Command in the Commission. We are told *How* to obey the Command in the Commission. Finally, we are told *Why* to obey the Command in the Commission. Let us give treatment to those questions, individually, one at a time.

WHO Is to Obey Our LORD'S Great Commission?

> **The *Church* was formed in Acts chapter two, when *all believers* were Spirit Baptized into the body of Christ.**

Every individual follower of the Lord Jesus Christ is responsible, directly to Him, to obey His Great Commission. This is found in the word *"YE."* In some translations, the text simply says, *Go therefore...* The plural form of *you* is assumed in the translation. It is critical that we always maintain *context* when studying the Bible. When we do this all debate is precluded and God's word is clear. Remember Jesus was talking to His individual followers, since the *church* hadn't been constituted when the Great Commission was given. The word *"Ye"* in the text literally means, in Greek, *Every One of You, or Each One of You.* Jesus was *not* talking to the *Church* as a group, but to *individual followers.* You see, the Great Commission was given in the gospels. The *Church* was formed in Acts chapter two, when *all believers* were Spirit Baptized into the body of Christ. 1 Corinthians 12:12,13 says, "By one Spirit were you all baptized into the body of Christ..." This Spiritual Baptism happens at the moment of salvation, and that's what makes you part of His *Body!* Spiritual Baptism is not some second work of grace, subsequent to your salvation, as some erroneously teach. If that were true, our Lord would have *two* bodies; one body would represent those who had *just been saved,* and the other body would represent *super Saints who have, subsequent to being saved, received Spiritual Baptism!* No, Paul wrote, "By one Spirit were (past tense-at the moment of salvation) *we all* (the *"we"* is all believers) baptized into one body, whether Jews or Greeks, whether slaves or free; and we were *all* made to drink one Spirit." Therefore, in context, this command was given to *every* person who claims to be a follower of Jesus Christ! If you profess Jesus Christ as LORD, He gave this command to you!

The Savior's Strategy, or Satan's Subtle Substitute

Remember this...wherever God builds a house of prayer, Satan also builds a chapel there, and it may be seen upon examination which has the larger congregation! For a moment, let's see how *Satan's Subtle Substitute* has been implemented in the church in place of the *Savior's Strategy!* According to the text, the *Savior's Strategy* is that each and every individual follower of His is to be engaged in advancing the fulfillment of the Great Commission. This strategy worked to perfection for the first two centuries. Then, came the Roman Emperor, Constantine, through whom Satan implemented his subtle substitute. Constantine decided that, if he was going to amalgamate, consolidate, his empire, he needed to implement a common, universal religion. According to the *Antiquities* of the first century Jewish Historian, Josephus, Constantine chose *Christianity* as that religion. Being attracted to Roman Catholicism, he believed that water baptism made one a Christian. Accordingly, he marched his soldiers through rivers of water to baptize them and make them *Christian.* Then he placed them over the churches.

168

Next, Constantine gathered up all of the Bibles wherever they were to be found. The only Bibles allowed were chained to the altar in Roman Catholic Cathedrals. Therefore, nobody could operate by the Savior's Strategy, nor the whole counsel of God, the written word of God, as there was no open, available revelation from God. History records that this condition was finally remedied by the ministry of William Tyndale centuries later, when he labored to produce the Bible in the language of the common people! The Roman Catholic worship services were conducted in Latin instead of the universal language of the day, which was Greek. This went on for more than a thousand years, and is referred to in Reformed circles as the *Devil's Millennium!*

Next, Constantine decreed that all babies, born in the empire, would be water baptized to make them *Christian.* In this way, in his mind, all citizens of the empire would be *Christian.* Did you ever wonder how the world was introduced, on a massive scale, to *Infant Baptism?* Consult the *Antiquities of Flavious Josephus.*

Constantine was far from finished tampering with the Bible and the Body of Christ. He decided that, since all other religions had their worship centers, Christianity was in need of the same. Again, according to Josephus, Constantine commissioned his mother to build 11 Christian *cathedrals or worship centers* throughout the known world of that day. The most elaborate of these was built on a hillside outside of Rome; That hillside was, and is still, called (in Latin) *Vaticanus.* Yes, it is known as the Vatican today. Though subtlety, the *church* became something that you *go to* instead of something that Christians *are.* You see, what you *go to* you can *leave,* but what you *are,* you *are* all of the time!

Next, Constantine divided the church along an imaginary *Ladder of Dedication.*

Missionaries

Pastors

Elders, Deacons, Others

The Laity, Everyone Else

There is no division between *Foreign* and *Home* missions!

The Body of Christ bought into this evil, hateful, mission-killing strategy! Therefore, at the top of that imaginary ladder, we've placed the career Foreign Missionary. We regard the Foreign Missionary as the *best Christian*, because he/she goes to the foreign field, sacrifices culture, customs, family, and finance to re-pre-sent Christ *out there* somewhere. As a result, we make the advancement of the fulfillment of the Great Commission his/her responsibility, and place him/her at the top of this imaginary *Ladder of Dedication.* I cannot tell you how egregious and hateful this division of the Body of Christ must be in the heart and mind of God! We have turned His Great Commission into a Foreign Missions text. You will not find any such division *anywhere* in the Bible. There is no division between *Foreign* and *Home* missions! That's somebody else's invention. Guess who? The enemy of men's souls! This strategy has resulted in the division of the Body of Christ along the imaginary *Ladder of Dedication.*

Pastors

> **The institutional church has made *crowd size* the measure of the success of the Pastor and the local Body of Christ!**

On the next *rung* of this imaginary *Ladder of Dedication*, we place the Pastor. We make advancement of the fulfillment of the Great Commission his responsibility, but we want him to do it according to our tradition. As a result, most Pastors honestly believe that they're making disciples when they preach each week. When the crowd is large, the preacher's face is all smiles - *skinnin and grinnin*. However, when the crowd is *comfortable,* the preacher's face reflects disappointment, despondency, and despair. A comfortable crowd is when the people can lay down end to end in the pews and there's still room! The institutional church has made *crowd size* the measure of the success of the Pastor and the local Body of Christ! By this unbiblical standard, a church can be ¼" deep, Spiritually, but is considered wildly *successful* as long as it is ½" mile wide *physically.* This is blasphemously seen as the measure of *Spiritual* success because there's a large facility and a huge crowd on Sunday morning! In the fall, nearly every Sunday morning, you will find, in a very large facility in Pittsburgh Pa, a crowd of 65,050. Heinz Field is literally a ½" mile wide! What do you have there Spiritually? Nothing! If this scenario is the biblical measure of success, Jesus was a total flop at every point in His ministry! He began with 12 (one of those was a devil), and He had about 500 true followers when He died! Fact: Because of the way He trained and equipped the 11 Apostles as world visionary, radically committed (to Him and His strategy), reproducing multipliers (of others in kind), you and I know and love Him! Here we sit, at the end of the earth from Jesus' earthly headquarters, talking about Him more than 2000 years after He ascended! These 11 Apostles didn't have cars, airplanes, internet, social media, Zoom, television, nor telephones. They only had "tell-a-person"! They didn't have the fax, but they had the facts, in context, which constitutes *truth!* Could there possibly be any more profound measure of the success and the validation of the *Savior's Strategy*?

To exacerbate the problem, the typical Pastor believes that he is *building the kingdom of God.* In Matthew 16:18 Jesus said, "I will build my church; and the gates of hell shall not prevail against it." He makes crystal clear that building the church, and thus the kingdom, is His responsibility. In other words, *"You (Pastor) keep your hands off My job! You make disciples and all else will be taken care of. I will build my church using the disciples that you make!"*

> **Making disciples cannot be done from the pulpit! Jesus did not do it that way; if we, do it that way, we will improve upon Him**

The Pastor of the ¼" deep x ½ mile wide institution will tell you that every time he preaches, he is making disciples, though ½ of the human race has never heard the name of Jesus Christ! He's preaching to thousands each week, yet this dire condition exists wherein multitudes are going to hell having never even heard the name of Jesus. Why? Making disciples cannot be done from the pulpit! Jesus did not do it that way; if we, do it that way, we will improve upon Him! Yes, Jesus preached to the crowd, but nothing of His strategy relied on preaching to a crowd. For example, tradition calls Matthew chapters 5-7 the *Sermon on The Mount.* Have you ever critically examined the beginning of this *sermon* in Matthew 5 verses 1&2? Matthew wrote, "When Jesus *saw* the crowds, *He* went up on the mountain; and *after He sat down, His disciples* came to Him. He opened His mouth and *began to teach them" (emphasis mine).* Please do not miss this. The antecedent for the word *them* is the word *disciples.* In the passage that contains Jesus' main concentrated body of teaching, He is not teaching the crowd, but rather, He sat down and taught His disciples! Think about it. He didn't have a pa system, nor microphone, nor bullhorn. How in the world would he attempt to indoctrinate 15-20 thousand people on a mountainside, in a seated position, using only His natural voice? No, the scripture says that Jesus sat down (typical posture of a teaching Jewish Rabbi), His disciples came to Him, and He opened His mouth and taught them!

> **I am not besmirching a strong pulpit ministry. A strong pulpit ministry is necessary. In the scripture, it is typically used to emerge potential disciples.**

I am not besmirching a strong pulpit ministry. A strong pulpit ministry is necessary. In the scripture, it is typically used to emerge potential disciples. However, a strong pulpit ministry is not enough. For example, Jonathan Edwards was a prolific preacher and author. He succeeded his venerable grandfather, Solomon Stoddard, as Pastor in North Hampton Church in New England. After two decades of prolific, local, national, and international ministry and writing, he was fired from the church by a vote of 10-1! Why? At the core was his failure, and the failure of his predecessor, to employ the *Savior's Strategy* of reproductive disciple making! Author's Note: Newenglandhistoricalsociety.com

> **Jesus did not attempt to disciple the *crowd*. Jesus did not attempt to disciple from a pulpit.**

Preaching is not enough to equip the Saints for the work of the ministry. *Preaching* is analogous to drilling holes in the side of a mountain of granite, placing dynamite in those holes, blowing it up, *and expecting polished statues to fall from the sky! Teaching-Discipling,* on the other hand, is like a skilled artisan taking his tools to that mountain, cutting out a chunk of that granite, and then carefully hammering, chiseling, and polishing until he has created a masterpiece. Ephesians 2:10 says, "For we are His workmanship created in Christ Jesus for good works, which God prepared beforehand so that we would walk in them." The Greek word translated *workmanship* is *poiema,* from which we get the English word *poem.* Such a masterpiece is not brought into being through preaching; it can only be done exactly the way that Jesus did it, through teaching in a *life-on-life* relationship! Jesus did not attempt to disciple the *crowd.* Jesus did not attempt to disciple from a pulpit. Jesus did not give His command to make disciples *only* to Pastors. Jesus has already told us that this is His command to each individual Christian, and has modeled for us how to obey the command. The *Savior's Strategy* is that each and every one of His followers be disciples, and one cannot be a disciple without, necessarily, making disciples! Which manner and method of operation do we find in the typical church at this point? Do we find a following of the *Savior's Strategy,* or are we following *Satan's Subtle Substitute?* Is there even any room for debate? How about this; is there any room for repentance? Let us continue with *Satan's*, I mean, *Constantine's Ladder of Dedication*.

Elders, Deacons, Other Leaders

Next, on this imaginary *Ladder of Dedication*, we place the, Elders, Deacons, and other church leaders, and we consider them *"exceptional"* Christians if they even remotely get involved in carrying out our Lord's final command! Unfortunately, most of these Christians are not living in obedience to the command to make disciples. One of the chief qualifications of an Elder (synonymous with Pastor and Overseer - Bishop) is the gift of *teaching*. In Paul's instruction to his primary disciple, Timothy, in 1 Timothy 3:2 he wrote, "An overseer, then must be above reproach, the husband of one wife (in the original language literally *a one-woman man!* No woman can meet these criteria.), temperate, prudent, respectable, hospitable *able to teach*" (emphasis mine). In the contemporary church, we find men who are labeled *Administrative Pastor, Pastor of Music, Pastor of Counseling,* who do not have the gift of teaching the word of God, and are not expected to do so! This unbiblical structure is also a part of *Satan's Subtle Substitute!*

These *Religious Professionals* on the first 3 rungs of this imaginary *Ladder of Dedication* are identified as *Clergy*. This really bad term does not appear in your New Testament. Despite this fact, at most worship centers they even have parking spots clearly marked with signs that say, *Clergy!*

"Laity" (everyone else)

> **The typical Christian thinks all he is to do is rut his way *to* the meeting place 2-3 times a week, try to be a *good Christian* (whatever that means), and bring money; Satan is *delighted* that he has that attitude!!!**

Finally, way down *below* the bottom rung of this imaginary *Ladder of Dedication*, we find the *lowly lay person*. He's convinced that he has no personal stake in carrying out our Lord's final command at all! He believes this to be the responsibility of the church *professionals*. He thinks that he's not skilled, trained, and motivated enough to represent Christ. The typical Christian thinks all he is to do is rut his way *to* the meeting place 2-3 times a week, try to be a *good Christian* (whatever that means), and bring money; Satan is *delighted* that he has that attitude!!! These are "fans of the faith". They sit and *polish the pews* and cheer on the Missionary, Pastor and other *religious professionals*. These people below the very bottom rung of this imaginary *Ladder of Dedication* are referred to as "Laity". This *Biblical* word simply means *people.*

This division of "Clergy" and "Laity" was given to us by Satan thru the Roman Emperor, Constantine. Satan convinced the *Clergy* that they were the only ones formally educated, trained, committed, and skilled enough to re-pre-sent Jesus Christ. He convinced the *Laity* that it was not formally educated, trained, committed, and skilled enough to re-pre-sent Jesus Christ. So, the *Clergy* is to do all the Spiritual warfare, do all the preaching, do all the teaching, and the *Laity* is to rut their way back and forth *to* the *auditorium* 2-3 times a week, cheer the *Clergy* on, and bring the money to finance the plans and programs that the *Clergy* comes up with. These plans usually swing small circles around small situations and small people with little or no true vision that matches the Great Commission. These plans are usually totally for the benefit of the people inside the institution. These plans are usually designed to keep the people consolidated, amalgamated, and happily thinking they're heavily engaged in something decidedly *Christian*. Because the *Laity* is involved up to their eyeballs in these plans, and not sold out in advancing the fulfillment of our Lord's Great Commission, *one half of the human race has never heard the name of Christ!* According to the foregoing history and evaluation of how the typical church today operates, I ask again, on which side does the typical church fall? Is the typical church following the *Savior's Strategy,* or does the typical church operate by *Satan's Subtle Substitute?* It is crystal clear that *Satan's Subtle Substitute* dominates operation of the local Body of Christ!

Back in the early 90's the United States fought in a war called "Operation Desert Storm". The Commander of the United States and Allied Forces was a man by the name of Norman Schwarzkopf. Question: What if all of the soldiers had supplied Norman with the best weaponry, the finest logistics, the absolute best intelligence on the enemy, but they (the soldiers) stayed in their tents, or on the sidelines, cheering and sent Norman out to fight the war alone? Is there any doubt about what the outcome would have been? Absolutely not! Norman would have been annihilated in the first few seconds! Yet, this is exactly the strategy being employed by the *Army of the Lord*!

I'm reminded of the story of the woman missionary who had been evacuated out of the orient when the threat of hostility surfaced between Japan and the United States. She relocated to a place in the Southern U.S. On the day Pearl Harbor was bombed, she came out of her apartment, and a neighbor, who professed to be a Christian, stopped her and asked, "What do you think of your 'Japs now?" She pulled herself up straight and replied, "MY Japanese are trusting in Christ and resting in the Grace of God. If you're talking about the Japanese soldiers that just bombed Pearl Harbor, they're not MY Japanese .... they're YOURS! They're the ones YOU ignored! They're the ones you made no attempt to reach with the gospel of Jesus Christ!" I highly recommend a book written by the flight leader of the assault on Pearl Harbor, Mitsuo Fuchida, entitled *From Pearl Harbor to Calvary.*

So, every Christian is to be involved in this by the direct command of the Lord Jesus Christ! I ask the question, based on the text and this assessment, on which side does the typical church fall? Are we following the *Savior's Strategy*, or are we operating heavily on the side of *Satan's Subtle Substitute*? Seems the answer is fairly evident! God help us!

WHAT Am I/You to Do?

> ***Converts* grow *old* in the Lord, and *Disciples* grow *up* in the Lord and *reproduce*.**

We are to "Make Disciples." We are not commanded to make *converts,* but *Disciples.* You see *Converts* grow *old* in the Lord, and *Disciples* grow *up* in the Lord and *reproduce.* If you *only* make *converts*, you are in disobedience to a direct command of God that carries the same force as the *Ten Commandments* or any other command God ever gave! So, a *Disciple* is a world visionary, world impacting, radically committed follower and learner, of Jesus Christ, and a *reproducer* of others in kind. I say he is a *reproducer* because one dare not call himself a *Disciple* of Christ and ignore the only command of marching orders that He ever gave directly to *each* of His followers! You see, this is the *only command* in the Great Commission. "Go" is not a command. In fact, Jesus assumes you're going, because in Greek, this is a present circumstantial participle .... *"going, or having gone." Baptizing* is not a command. It too is a participle. *Teaching them to obey all things that I have commanded you* is not a command. *"Make Disciples"* is the only command, the only imperative mood verb, in the Great Commission! The Greek word translated "make disciples" is *matheteusate.* This is the only verb of command in the Great Commission. The other three main verbs modify the command, so they take on the force of the command. However, *make disciples* is the only command.

> ## It takes a disciple to make a disciple

It is impossible to obey this command without also being a disciple. Genesis 1:11 places a lock on this principle. It says, "Everything will reproduce after his own kind." Therefore, it takes a disciple to make a disciple. Now, you may ask how this principle was confirmed in Jesus. He made disciples. Since it takes a disciple to make a disciple, what did this look like in His life? Turn your Bible to Isaiah 50:4-6, which reads, "The Lord God has given Me the tongue of disciples, that I may know how to sustain the weary one with a word. He awakens Me morning by morning. He awakens My ear to listen as a disciple. The Lord God has opened My ear; and I was not disobedient nor did I turn back. I gave My back to those who strike Me, and My cheeks to those who pluck out the beard; I did not cover My face from humiliation and spitting." If you have a good annotated Bible, you will notice that every first person pronoun is capitalized. Why? This is Jesus speaking, through Isaiah, in eternity past! This was written a minimum 700 years before Jesus came into His creation at Bethlehem! It is no wonder that He would make disciples when He came to earth, because He had been one in eternity past! It takes a disciple to make a disciple! Further, because of obedience to His command, a disciple of Christ will necessarily turn people into disciples, otherwise that person forfeits the right to be called His disciple!

What Did It Mean When Jesus Commanded these men to "Make Disciples"?

> **The Bible cannot mean today what it didn't mean to the people who originally received that word.**

The Bible cannot mean today what it didn't mean to the people who originally received that word. Context is always an imperative in the reading, studying, and proclamation of the word of God. What did these 11 men hear when Jesus commanded them to *Make Disciples*? This concept has deep roots in Jewish culture; since this is the culture that Jesus was humanly born into, it is obvious that God painted a picture by ordaining this concept, this process, in the Jewish culture. In order to truly understand what this means; we must establish the *cultural context*. In the Jewish culture, the

180

children started primary school at about age 5, and continued there thru age 12. During this time, they were required to memorize the Torah (the first 5 books of the Old Testament) ... all of it! At age 12, or after the first menstrual cycle, the girls were offered for marriage. The boys continued, but at this level of their education, (Beth Talmud) they were now to learn the meaning of the scripture they'd spent years memorizing.

Now, you must also know that, in Jewish Culture, the Rabbi was/is revered. It was every young boy's dream to *follow*, or be the Talmid (Hebrew term for "Disciple") of a respected Rabbi. These Talmidim (plural) had only one purpose and goal in life; that was to be exactly like the Rabbi in his walk with God. These Talmidim (plural Hebrew form of Disciple) watched their Rabbi like a hawk. They followed him everywhere. If he went to the toilet, they would wait outside for him to emerge, because they knew when he came out that he would pray, and they wanted to hear that prayer! I highly recommend seeing the movie *Fiddler on the Roof* where is beautifully illustrated. For example, when the Rabbi emerged from the toilet, he would typically thank the God of the universe for "the openings in our bodies." (We hear that and laugh, because it seems silly to us. However, *let one of those openings in your body stop working and you'll NOT find it any longer a laughing matter!*) The goal of any Talmid was not merely to know what the Rabbi knew. It was much stronger than that. His goal was to be exactly like the Rabbi in his walk with God! The Jews understood that when a Talmid asked to *follow* a Rabbi, he was asking *can I be like you by learning your walk with God?* In fact, the common description of a good Talmid was that he would be "covered by the dust of his Rabbi's feet". In other words, as the Rabbi walked down a dusty Palestinian path, the Talmid would be following so closely that he would actually be covered by the dust kicked up by the Rabbi's feet! This history is the basis of this book's title.

Since it was every Jewish boy's dream to become like (follow) a respected Rabbi, between the ages of 12 and 15, while studying in "Beth Talmud" a young "would be" Talmid would look for a Rabbi to "follow". The Talmid would *choose* the Rabbi that he wanted to be like in his walk with God. Jesus turned this practice on its head, as we will see later. When the would be Talmid had settled on one, he would ask that Rabbi the question, "Rabbi may I follow you?" The Rabbi would be humbled and honored by the question. Then, it would get serious. The Rabbi would typically give the young man a test, or tests, to determine whether the young man had what was necessary to "be like him". For example, the Rabbi may ask the young man to recite the book of Deuteronomy. That would be no problem, as the young man would have learned that in primary school. Next the Rabbi may ask, "In the book of Amos, the prophet takes 17 phrases from the book of Deuteronomy and turns them into 17 prophecies. Give me the 17 phrases and the corresponding 17 prophecies." When the young man could only quote 16 of these phrases and prophecies, the Rabbi would give him a decision. He would say, "My son, you are a godly young man. You know Torah. However, God has not given you what it takes to *be like me!* Go and live for God. Be a godly fisherman. Or, be a godly carpenter. *But you do not have what it takes.*

It is important that you not miss the ramifications of what I just told you. In order that you don't, allow a breakdown.

First, because these young men (the Disciples of Jesus) had already begun their secular professions, they had most certainly (in all likelihood) been rejected by a Rabbi.

Secondly, because of the culture and school system, these young men were likely between the ages of 12-15. This would exclude Simon Peter, who was likely older. If you check Matthew 17 (verse 24 and following) you'll find a story about "taxation". Careful study reveals that the law required every Jewish male 20 years of age or older to pay a "Temple Tax" (Exodus 30:13-14; 2 Chronicles 24:9). Of all of the Disciples, why was it only Simon Peter who was required to pay the tax? Obviously, he was the only one of age to meet the requirement for taxation! Scripture also tells us that Peter had a "Mother-In-Law". In the culture, young men typically married around age 20. Therefore, we conclude, that our Christian pictures and artifacts depicting the Apostles as old men with grey beards is wrong! With the exception of Simon Peter, they were likely teenagers!

> **Jesus broke with the culture in that His Talmidim did not choose Him, but rather, He chose them!**

Thirdly, Jesus broke with the culture in that His Talmidim did not choose Him, but rather, He chose them! In John 15 Jesus tells His Talmidim, "You have not chosen Me, but I have chosen you, and ordained you, that you should go and bear fruit and that your fruit should remain" (John 15:16). Most Commentators will tell you that this great verse is dealing with the Doctrine of "Election". However, it is inconsistent that Jesus would be teaching on "Fruit-Bearing" and in the midst of doing so, drop in one verse about *Soteriology* (Doctrine of Salvation) and talk about God's *Election of people for salvation!* That would be like teaching on the ordinance of *Baptism* for an hour and close the teaching by saying, "Now, a few words on giving!" No, this verse is about Disciple Making! Matthew 4:18-20 says, "Now, as Jesus was walking by the Sea of Galilee, He saw two brothers, Simon who was called Peter, and Andrew his brother, casting a net into the sea; for they were fishermen. And He said to them, *Follow Me and I will make you fishers of men. Immediately they left their nets and followed Him.*"

> **It was *every* young man's dream and life's ambition to have the privilege of being the Talmid of a storied Rabbi.**

Matthew 4:21, 22 says, "Going on from there He saw two other brothers, James the son of Zebedee, and John his brother, in the boat with Zebedee, their father, mending their nets; and He called them. Immediately they left the boat and their father, and followed Him." I have heard many a sermon on Zebedee. Many go into great detail about how Zebedee must have felt abandoned by his sons, who left him with all of the work of the fishing business to go hang out with this Rabbi. If you know the cultural context, then you know that is absurd! In the culture it was *every* young man's dream and life's ambition to have the privilege of being the Talmid of a storied Rabbi. It is therefore not a stretch, nor reading into the text, to understand that, while his sons had previously been rejected, he (Zebedee) was also once a young man rejected by a Rabbi that he desired to be like! In that culture, the fishing business was most assuredly plan B. Zebedee was, no doubt, beaming with pride and joy that this storied, miracle working, Rabbi had specifically chosen his sons for this great honor!

In Luke 5:27, 28, the scripture says, "After that He went out and noticed a tax collector named Levi sitting in the tax booth, and He said to him, Follow Me. And he left everything behind and got up and began to follow Him." This man had obviously been previously rejected by a Rabbi, and had bought-in (literally, because he had to purchase the job) to being a hated tax collector! In other words, he went from desiring to be like a storied Rabbi to engaging in a profession that made him one of the most despised people in all of Israel!

> **This is the *Savior's Strategy;* we are to turn every available person into what He turned those 11 men into.**

To sum it up, in the Jewish culture, a Talmid had to be a radically committed learner, follower, an apprentice, faithful, available, and trainable pursuer of the lifestyle of the Rabbi; this *Talmid/Disciple* would necessarily reproduce others in kind. This is what the 11 Disciples of Jesus understood when Jesus gave His Great Commission that included the command to *Make Disciples.* This is the *Savior's Strategy;* we are to turn every available person into what He turned those 11 men into.

Satan's Subtle Substitute

Now, what is Satan's Subtle Substitute at this point? Instead of producing the type of person described above, the institution is delighted if it's members simply invite people to the auditorium where the Church meets. The leaders of the institution are overjoyed if one of its members actually shares the gospel. The Pew Research Center, estimates that 1 in 5 Christians even look for ways to share their faith with anyone in today's environment. 70% of all Christians believe they are truly practicing Christianity if they attend corporate worship 3 out of 4 Sundays per month. 57% of all Christians believe that whatever *religion* a person follows is perfectly fine and it is just a matter of personal choice! Satan must be gleeful about these numbers!

Next, Satan is delighted if a Christian is wrapped around the idea of *only* making *converts.* Now, immediately, some will say, "How could you possibly criticize the making of converts?" I am not criticizing that, but if it stops there, one is still in radical disobedience of the only command of marching orders that Jesus ever gave to His followers. He did not say, "Go therefore and *make converts...*" He said, "Go and *make disciples...*"! Again, *converts* grow old in the Lord; *disciples* (after the model Jesus reproduced) grow up in the Lord and reproduce others in kind. Instead of following the command of Jesus, so many are enamored with *notching the belt* with the number of *decisions or professions of faith* they were able to extract from people! After all, getting people to mouth "the sinner's prayer" (if someone could only give me the scripture reference for that) or make a *decision for Christ* is far easier and infinitely less time and resource consuming than *life on life transference!* Again, Satan must be delighted with this, as it facilitates his subtle substitute in place of the Savior's Strategy.

> **Finally, Satan's Subtle Substitute is fully realized when believers are sold-out on simply being a *good Christian***

Finally, Satan's Subtle Substitute is fully realized when believers are sold-out on simply being a *good Christian*. He loves *fans of the faith, polishers of the pews, or* folks focused on being *active in the church* (whatever that means). I know a brother who told me that he's *very active* in his local church, as he's part of the *snow removal ministry!* Another Brother told me that he's heavily involved in the *auto repair ministry.* Yet another brother told me that he is part of the *Usher Ministry* of his church. I know a lady who sees her *ministry* as making the bread that is served at communion! How sinfully distant from Jesus' command in the commission are all of these activities when compared with what the 11 heard in Matthew 28:16-20! Yes, I did say "sinfully", as all disobedience (be it co-mission or o-mission is sin) to the command of the King is sin! Dawson Trotman, founder of The Navigators, used to say, "Activity is no substitute for production. Production is no substitute for reproduction." I asked, tongue-in-cheek, on which side does the typical church land; on the side of the *Savior's Strategy,* or on the side of *Satan's Subtle Substitute?*

WHERE Are We to Make Disciples?

ALL NATIONS! In Greek the phrase is ***Ta Ethnae,*** which means *all ethnic groups!* We are to constantly enlarge our vision to include *all nations!* John 3:16 tells us *"For God so loved the world."* Not just Harrisburg, Pa, Detroit MI, London England, Seoul South Korea, Johannesburg South Africa, Beijing China, or the USA, but *the whole wide world!* According to Colossians 1:9, Spiritual "Vision" is seeing things from God's point of view. Proverbs 29:18 tells us, "Where there is no vision (seeing things from God's point of view) the people perish." People are God's highest creation signature, as we are made in His image. So, God's most precious commodity perishes where there is no seeing things from His perspective! Since God's heart is for the whole wide world of people, this is a very serious matter! If your heart is not to see the whole world know Jesus, and if you're not mapping and implementing His strategy to accomplish that vision, your perspective is out of step with God's!

> **I have a question for you at this point. If God were to answer *ALL* of your *PERSONAL* prayers, what would be the effect on the total global cause of Christ?**

I have a question for you at this point. If God were to answer *ALL* of your *PERSONAL* prayers, what would be the effect on the total global cause of Christ? When you answer that question honestly before God, you will see the limit of your vision. *Remember we're talking about Jesus' final instructions (command) to us HIS followers!*

God here is telling us to enter *all* of the field. Your family, your church, your community, your city, your state, your country is not enough! Matthew 13:38 says, "The field is the world." The *world* begins where your toes end! Wherever people exist that do not have

187

an opportunity to hear, understand, and respond to the gospel of Jesus Christ is my responsibility, and it is equally *your* responsibility. I am, you are, to implement Jesus' strategy to make Disciples of all ethnic groups. Someone, will say, "That's an impossible task!" I remind you that Jesus did it; yet He never traveled more than 90 miles from home and in that He was carried as an infant! Now what's the argument? Oh, I know. Some thinking person will say, "Yeah, but He was God." True, but He didn't do it as God. He lived on earth as a faith-dependent, believing man. He clearly, over and over, said, "I do nothing of myself." Philippians chapter 2:5-8 tells us that Jesus laid aside His independent use of His divine rights and privileges and functioned as a man; He was 100% God and 100% man, and yet still only 100%! As man we see Him lying in the bottom of the boat exhausted and requiring sleep. As God, we see Him rise from that same sleep and speak to the waves and the sea obeys His voice. He didn't implement His strategy of reaching the whole world through His direct use of His divine power. No! He implemented His strategy as a man to show us exactly how to do the same. What was that strategy? He trained and equipped 12 men (by divine appointment one of them was a devil) and because of the way He comprehensively trained those 11 men His name travels on the lips of all ethnic groups on earth! My Discipler, Herb Hodges used to say, "Jesus saw the masses through the man, and then He trained and equipped the man to impact the masses."

John 3:16 is likely the most popular verse (universally) in the New Testament. It does not say, "For God so loved my church that He gave…" Nor does it say, for God so loved my city that He gave…" It doesn't say, "For God so loved my *community* that He gave…" It doesn't say, "For God so loved the United States of America that He gave…" News flash…God is *not* an American! God is nothing but glory, and it is manifested everywhere, but *Old Glory* (nickname of the US Flag) is *not* draped over the throne of almighty God! No! The verse says, "For God so loved the *world* that He gave His only begotten Son, that whosoever believes in Him shall not perish, but have eternal life." Jesus' *strategy* for reaching all ethnic groups in the world with this wonderful news is clearly delineated in our primary text found in Matthew 28:16-20, wherein He commands us to make disciples of all ethnic groups. You must first reach them with the good news, and once they've responded to this good news, I/you are to "teach them to observe all things whatsoever I (Jesus) have commanded you (me)." That includes the command for them to "go and make disciples of all ethnic groups." So, you are commanded to turn people of all ethnic groups into the same thing that Jesus turned the 11 into. They were turned into radically committed followers, equally committed learners, of Jesus Christ, who were world-visionary, world-impacting, reproducing multipliers of others in kind! Notice that He did not command us to go into all the world and make *converts* of all ethnic groups; The making of *converts* is inherently covered in the command to make disciples! It is impossible to make a disciple of one who has not been converted to Jesus Christ! So, the command to *make disciples of all ethnic groups* covers all that is required for gospel advance. That is the *Savior's Strategy* for reaching the world of lost humanity with the good news of the gospel!

Satan's Subtle Substitute

The enemy of men's souls, Satan, always has a *Subtle Substitute* at every point to counteract the *Savior's Strategy*. What is *Satan's Subtle Substitute* at this point? He subtly induces the hellish idea of *self-centered* Christianity. What does that look like? The local body turns all of the strength of its drives in on itself. So, everything is done for the betterment, the comfort, the entertainment of the people inside. IF any discipling is done, it is the discipling to substitutes like *local church growth*. So, we implore members to invite their friends and family to the place where the church meets in order to build numbers.

We pound the idea that *we must reach our community for Christ.* In order to do this, many "church-based organizations" (I hesitate to call some by the word *church)* canvas with community surveys, going door to door, to ask *unchurched Charley and Charlene* what would draw them to the building where the church meets. Then, they go back and adapt their style of worship to match the results of the survey! They reject doctrinally accurate worship songs, hire skilled musicians (regardless of their Spiritual condition) to crank up the *Christian-Lite* Rock & Roll sound, turn down the ceiling lights, fire up the smoke machine, and replace the expositional proclamation of the word of God with 15-minute *sermonettes* that touch the trending online social issue of the day. This draws numbers of people, which brings in much more money, which buys bigger buildings, coffeehouses, gymnasiums, baseball fields, and many forms of entertainment for the people inside, and enticement for the people outside to join the club!

The members who perform the surveys, man the coffeehouses, gymnasiums, baseball fields, praise bands, etc. are commended by the leadership on being *active in the church and doing the work of the Lord!* Meanwhile, the *Savior's Strategy* goes wanting, and the *world* tragically goes into eternity without God! Oh, occasionally the church will have a *Missions Sunday* where they select a focus country, hang up maps, don the traditional dress and eat the traditional food found there, and say a prayer for that country. Then, they go back to *church-life* as usual because they've checked the *missions* box. This is very much akin to attempting to *Christianize* the local Kiwanis Club! This is just one prong of *Satan's Subtle Substitute!* Again, I ask, does the typical church operate according to the *Savior's Strategy,* or does its operation look more like *Satan's Subtle Substitute?*

WHEN Are We to Make Disciples?

Remember, I said the word "Go" is translated *as you are going* in Greek. In other words, Jesus is saying, "Do not take one more step. When you move your feet, I want you advancing the fulfillment of this command!" The world begins where your toes end! As you, while you, since you are going. The "going" is not necessarily a matter of geographical distance. The frontier to be crossed is one of *gospel awareness.* In other words, the question is do the people have the opportunity to hear, understand, and respond to the gospel of Jesus Christ? Go therefore! You can translate that word, *go,* into Greek, Ugaritic, Syriac, Aramaic, or any other language and it still means the same thing.... GO! It's a synonym for *Don't Stay*! It's God's way of saying, "Break the huddle and get into the game!" You see, you don't pay $125 or more per head to go to a National Football League contest to watch the team huddle! No! You go to see them get out of the huddle and into the game! And, this is God's way of saying "Break the huddle! Get into the game!"

Unfortunately, because of our 'safety-first, consumer-friendly, Genie-in-a-bottle' attitude toward what Christianity is about, the church has become something of a *"Holy Huddle".* We huddle frequently and recite 'game plans, chalk talk, and raise passionate discussions about reaching the lost. Then we pray that the Lord will reach the Lost, adjourn, and then come back together to recite game plans, chalk talk and raise passionate discussions about reaching the lost! What's usually missing is any serious examination of Jesus' *strategy* for reaching the lost, and any appreciable *implementing action* in pursuing that strategy. Thus, we *huddle* and give more attention to counting *nickels and noses, or to the killer b's...buildings, bodies, budgets, and bulletins,* than we do in pursuing the mandate, method, and model of the *Savior's Strategy* for reaching the lost.

Maybe you've seen the placard on an office wall that says, "The main thang is to keep the main thang the main thang!" The making of disciples after the model the Master left for us is not a hobby! It is not a part-time endeavor. It involves all of life all of the time! Obedience to the command of our Lord "as you are going make disciples of all ethnic groups" is a *lifestyle enterprise!* Lord please open the eyes of our hearts and flood them with light so that we can see things from YOUR point of view (Ephesians *1:18-23)!*

Satan's Subtle Substitute

What is *Satan's Subtle Substitute* at this point? Maintain the huddle, recite chalk talk, and subtly change the mindset from *go and tell, to come and hear!* I once heard a Deacon in a church tell his son, who was fired up about going to Kenya to help disciple Pastors, "If God wants those people to know about Him, He will send somebody else to tell them. We have enough lost people here at home to worry about!"

I'm reminded of the brutal training Jesus did with Simon Peter in Matthew 16:21- 23. "From that time Jesus began to show His disciples that He must go to Jerusalem, and suffer many things from the elders and chief priests and scribes, and be killed, and be raised up on the third day. Peter took Him aside and began to rebuke Him, saying, God forbid it, Lord! This shall never happen to You. But He turned and said to Peter, Get behind Me Satan! You are a stumbling block to Me, for you are not setting your mind on God's interests, but man's." Peter showed more interest in Satan's program (trying to keep the *Seed of the woman* from crushing his head) than God's plan of bringing salvation to men!

Satan's Subtle Substitute is to totally *localize* the attention and efforts of the church, yes and of the Christian! What about you? I'm not talking, here, about your church, your Pastor, your church leadership, but you! Do you share the attitude that we have *plenty of lost people right here at home, so why would we spend all of those resources to go way over there to make disciples?"* In Acts 1:8, Jesus said, "You shall be witnesses unto Me both in Jerusalem, and in Judea, and in Samaria, and in the uttermost parts of the world." Simultaneously, that is to be our sphere of disciple-making influence. When He commanded you to, go into all the world and *make disciples* He knew that the world *begins where your toes end!* This is why He said, "as you are going..." I ask the rhetorical question, on which side does the typical Christian fall – on the side of the *Savior's Strategy, or on the side of Satan's Subtle Substitute?*

HOW Are We to Make Disciples?

We are to make Disciples by *going, baptizing, and teaching.* We've already examined *going,* so let's look at the other two, respectively.

What is baptism?

Let's consider the word *Baptizing.*

The word *"Baptizing"* doesn't merely mean *Get them wet!* But, when we're told to "Baptize them into the name of the Father, the Son, and the Holy Spirit", we are being told to *identify them with the triune God of the Bible.* Christian baptism is a symbol of that truth. When the Holy Spirit spoke in Acts 2:38, speaking through Peter, "Repent and be baptized," He gave a command there to the individual who repents and believes.

So, the church is commanded to baptize. The individual is commanded to be baptized. There is really no lack of clarity with regard to this. In fact, in each of the cases where the great commission is given, in Matthew, Mark, and Luke, there's an emphasis on baptism. In spite of this, there is widespread noncompliance with what is a very simple modifier of the command to make disciples. Again, *baptizing* is not a command, but since it modifies a command, it takes on the same force of that command. In many ways, this is sort of the easiest act of obedience that a Christian can do, because all the rest have to do with sorting out the stuff that's in your mind and heart, for the most part. This simple act, when obediently done, demonstrates a heart that seeks to honor the Word of the Lord.

What are we talking about here when we talk about baptism? Simply, here's a definition: it is a ceremony by which a person is immersed into water. There are two Greek verbs that are used in the New Testament with regard to baptism—they are translated baptism": *bapto* and *baptizo*—*bapto* is the less common, used only four times in the New Testament and it means "to dip into". In fact, it was used for "dyeing" when you immerse something in a dye. It's the word *immerse...bapto. Baptizo* is an intensified form of *bapto*. The Greeks had ways of sticking in a few extra letters and intensifying a word. In fact, the terms *bapto* and *baptizo*, the verb, and *baptismas*, the noun, could have been translated *immerse* and probably would have solved a lot of problems, but the translators chose to transliterate (bring the word from one language over letter for letter into the new language) the Greek *baptizo* into "baptise." It means *to immerse*.

The Greeks had a totally different word for *sprinkling*, and that word, *rhantisanti*, is used of "sprinkling or splattering with water". It's a different word altogether. We're not talking about *sprinkling*. There's no such thing as a ceremony of sprinkling in the Bible, or pouring or any application of water to the individual. Whenever you find "baptism" in the Bible, it is the word "immerse" or "submerse" and it means "putting the person under the water." This is so obvious that even John Calvin, who literally believed in infant baptism through sprinkling, touts' emersion as the only valid method of baptism in his writing.

In Matthew 3:6, we read about an account of the ministry of John the Baptist. The text says, "They were being baptized by him in the Jordan River."

In Matthew 3:16 we read, "After being baptized, Jesus," having been baptized, "went up immediately, (literally) out of the water." In order for Jesus to go "up out of the water" He first would have to go down into the water. Submersion is clearly in view.

In John 3:2 we see the same pattern. When John the Baptist was doing his baptizing, he picked a place at the Jordan River that was deep. It says, "John was baptizing in Anon, near Salem (Of all the spots you could stop along the Jordan River, he picked that one.

Why?) there was much water there." This is simply another way of saying the water was deep enough to get them under. Here again, submersion is the mode depicted.

In Mark, chapter 1, verse 5, submersion is in view. "All the country of Judea was going out to him and all the people of Jerusalem, they were being baptized by him in the Jordan River"..."in the Jordan River."

In Acts 8:36, we read about the scene of what happened when Philip came across the Ethiopian eunuch and led him to Christ. The Eunuch said, "Look; water! What prevents me from being baptized"? Then, in verse 38 we read, "he ordered the chariot to stop, they both went down into the water, and he immersed him." It couldn't be clearer that submersion is in view; the text even says so.

Why did Jesus submit to water baptism? In doing so, Jesus is simply saying, *"In order to fulfill all righteousness, I will be obedient to what God desires. If I'm going to live as a man, I'm going to obey all the commands."* Therefore, in submitting to baptism, Jesus is showing us how critical obedience is. Obedience is so critical that He did it, even though there was no need for Him to go through any kind of cleansing, any kind of repentance, any kind of confession of sin.

In our text, Matthew 28:19 says, "Baptizing them in the name of the name of the Father, and the Son, and the Holy Spirit." First, this is not some liturgical formula. In fact, this is the only place where you have this statement. In other texts, you see baptism in the name of Jesus, or into Jesus Christ. *Eis* (Greek) can be translated *in or into.* We often use this statement when we baptize. We are identifying the obedient one with the *Triune* God of the Bible! Here, we see the Trinity in view.

Deuteronomy 6:4 (Shema') says, "Hear oh Israel. The LORD is thy God. The LORD is one. Love the LORD your God with all your heart, with all of your soul, and with all of your might." There are two Hebrew words for *one*. They are *yachid* and *Echad*. The word used here is *Echad,* and it means *Compound Oneness, or oneness in unity!* So, this is an emphasis on the Trinity. Back to our text, in Matthew 28:19. Here Jesus is absolutely stating that He is God! One in unity with the Father and the Holy Spirit!

> **So, we are to identify with the Triune God of the Bible; this pictures the death, burial, and resurrection of Jesus Christ**

So, we are to identify with the Triune God of the Bible; this pictures the death, burial, and resurrection of Jesus Christ. Now in Harrisburg Pa on 18th and State Street, that wouldn't cause much of a stir. However, when you identified yourself as a follower of that hated Nazarene Carpenter, the Lord Jesus Christ, in Palestine, you risked everything! You would be ejected from the synagogue, which was the absolute center of Jewish life. Your family and friends would disown you. If you had a business nobody would do business with you anymore. You were, basically, shunned!

So, we see the Savior's Strategy, in the commission, is that the discipler is to baptize. What does that mean? There are a great many people that will tell you that when you emphasize the command to make disciples you are excluding evangelism. Nowhere does the Bible teach the baptizing of anyone who has not repented and turned to the Lord Jesus Christ for salvation! So, when Jesus said we are to make disciples by baptizing as one of the functions, that means that evangelism is necessarily included.

Satan's Subtle Substitute

What is Satan's Subtle Substitute at this point? Some denominations make baptism the capstone of salvation! In other words, if you repent and turn to Jesus Christ for salvation, your conversion is incomplete, and you are not saved, until you are baptized in water. The Bible nowhere teaches or even suggests this! I offer just one example; the thief on the cross. In Luke 23, one of the criminals crucified alongside Jesus repented and acknowledged Jesus as "Lord". In verses 42 and 43 we read, "And he was saying, Jesus remember me when you come in Your kingdom! And He (Jesus) said to him, Truly I say to you, today you shall be with Me in Paradise." Notice, that Jesus didn't order His disciples to try and get this man down and baptize him! He said, "today you'll be with me in Paradise." Baptism is not required for salvation; it is a matter of obedience, which always results in blessing!

Satan has really gotten his hooks into the church on the matter of baptism! Some make it the capstone of salvation, while others, such as the Quakers, don't baptize at all. They say that it is purely *mechanical,* and therefore unnecessary.

> **In the typical denominational tradition, who is authorized to baptize? Right…the Pastor. Is the Great Commission given only to *Pastors?***

Don't miss this part. In the typical denominational tradition, (ugly word) who is authorized to baptize? Right…the Pastor. Is the Great Commission given only to *Pastors?* Then, what does that mean? "Baptizing them in the name of the Father, and the Son, and the Holy Ghost" is not a command, but it modifies the command. That means that it carries the same force as the command. That means that God authorizes you, Believer, Discipler, to perform the ordinance of Baptism!

A scriptural example is in order here. In Acts 6:5, Philip was one of the 7 men, all with Greek names – strongly suggesting that they were Hellenistic Jews, chosen by the church as servants. That's what a *Deacon* is. Even the etymological derivation of the word *deacon* tells us this. In Greek, *dia* means through. *Konos* (root form of the second half of the word) means *to kick dust*. A Deacon is a person who is so hot-hearted to serve that he kicks up a column of dust behind him on his way to serve! He is not a *clout functionary*, responsible for leading and directing the affairs of the church, making decisions on money, giving direction to the Pastor, etc. He is a servant of the people of God! These 7 were to make certain that the problem involving the daily administration to the Hellenistic widows was taken care of. The Apostles laid hands on these men as a symbolic affirmation of approval in appointing them to this work of distributing goods and sustenance. They were servants. Philip was one of these 7 men.

> **Notice, the Christians were scattered, but the preachers were allowed to remain in Jerusalem.**

In Acts 8, the Lord sent a persecution to the Jerusalem church, beginning with the stoning of Stephen. This bears witness to the seriousness in our Lord's statement of the Great Commission found in Acts 1:8. There He said, "You shall be witnesses unto Me, both in Jerusalem, and in all Judea, and in Samaria, and even to the remotest part of the earth." Acts 8:1 reads thus, "Saul was in hearty agreement with putting him (Stephen) to death. And on that day a great persecution began against the church in Jerusalem, and they were all scattered throughout the regions of Judea and Samaria, except the Apostles." Notice, the Christians were scattered, but the preachers were allowed to remain in Jerusalem. Verse 4 of the same chapter says, "Therefore, those who had been scattered went about preaching the word." This is how Christianity spread across the known world of that day; every believer went about preaching the gospel! Christianity is *not* a preacher's movement! Ephesians 4:11, 12 tells us that the preacher's job is to equip the Saints for the work of the ministry!

Philip was among *those who had been scattered that went about preaching the word.* Philip went down to the city of Samaria, to the half-breed Jews, and preached the gospel of Jesus Christ to them. Acts 8:5 says, "Philip went down to the city of Samaria and began proclaiming Christ to them." Philip's preaching kicked off a great move of God in salvation among the Samaritans. However, in the midst of this great awakening, God told Philip to leave there! You may wonder, why God would do this in the midst of such fruitful ministry that He had given this man. God had bigger plans! In Acts 8:28-35 we see God's plan, that was bigger than Samaria, included introduction of the gospel to the African Continent! God sent Philip to an Ethiopian Eunuch, a court official of Candace, queen of the Ethiopians, who was in charge of all her treasure! This man was one click under the Queen of Ethiopia! He was, obviously, a Jewish proselyte as verse 27 tells us that "...he had come to Jerusalem to worship." Philip preached Jesus to him from Isaiah 53, and God opened the eyes of his heart to saving faith in the Lord Jesus Christ! Immediately, verse 36 says, "As they went along the road they came to some water; and the eunuch said, Look! Water! What prevents me from being baptized? And Philip said If you believe with all your heart, you may. And he answered and said, I believe that Jesus Christ is the Son of God. And he ordered the chariot to stop; and they both went down into the water, Philip as well as the eunuch, and he baptized him."

Philip, one of the *servants* identified in Acts 6:5, baptized this man as the representative of the body of Christ! Someone will say, "But Philip was an Evangelist!" Yes, but he was not recognized as such until he was recognized as such in Acts 21:8. In fact, he is the first missionary named in scripture and the first to be given the title *Evangelist.* However, when he preached the gospel to the Eunuch and baptized him, Philip carried no such title! He was a member of the body of Christ that was scattered abroad in the persecution, while the preachers were left in Jerusalem.

Like the staccato beating of a drum, I ask this question at this point, "On which side does the typical church fall – on the side of the Savior's Strategy, or on the side of Satan's Subtle Substitute?" Is there really any question?

Teaching them to obey all that I have commanded you

Now, look at the phrase "Teaching them to observe all things I have commanded you." Once we have "Gone" and taken the message to them, and identified them with the triune God of the Bible through Christian Baptism, then we are to teach them the word of God line-upon-line, precept-upon-precept. Leading them to faith in Jesus Christ is just the beginning; That is the tip of the iceberg in fulfilling His command to Make Disciples. At that point you've made a *convert*, but the command is to *Make Disciples.*

Far too often, in our churches, we see someone come weeping their way to Jesus, we stand them up in front of the Body and shout *Hallelujah,* and when the Amen is said, we bid them farewell and see you next week. Would any mother ever even think of giving birth to a baby and then placing that baby on the doorstep and saying, "See you next week"? No! Yet we do that to *newborn baby Christians* on a routine basis and think nothing of it. If we do *teach* them, it usually begins with *giving,* or *how to be a good (fill in the blank with Baptist, Methodist, Presbyterian, etc.).* We act as if, through osmosis, that newborn will pick up all they need to know about living the Christian life, grace, sin, confession, forgiveness, the importance of a daily quiet time, prayer, and the Great Commission of our Lord! Then we look with bewilderment (or *Phariseeism)* when that newborn stumbles and falls in frustration and defeat!!! Could it be that God doesn't give more *newborns* because we are not very good *mothers?* To paraphrase Augustine:

No man can call God his father without the church as his mother. If we earnestly, with reckless abandonment, follow the command to *Make Disciples* these problems will be automatically eliminated in "Teaching them to observe all things I have commanded you…"

What we've said so far is crucially, critically, important. However, believe this, what is said next is of even greater importance to you as a follower of the LORD Jesus Christ! You might question how I can make such a statement. I say this because the *why* is the capstone of everything about you as a Christian!

WHY Are We to Make Disciples Of All Nations?

Matthew 28:18 says, *"All authority is given unto me in heaven and in earth. THEREFORE..."* Do you see what I see? Verse 19 depends on verse 18! When you see the word *therefore* it refers to something that comes before. What comes before? Jesus makes an astounding statement! *"All authority in heaven and earth has been given to Me!*

What right does HE have to make such a "categorical" statement? He can state this because of *who* He is and *what* He has done! Jesus Christ is God almighty, God in the flesh, KING OF KINGS, AND LORD OF LORDS! He died on Calvary's cross for our sins, rose again the third day and ascended to the right hand of the Father. He ever lives to make intercession for us. He's coming back again for us, His church. He will reign King of Kings and Lord of Lords. He has every right to say, "I am the one who is in control in the physical realm, and the Spiritual realm - everywhere and anywhere!!! I AM LORD!!!"

> **Rule #1: There is only ONE God.**
> **Rule #2: You are NOT Him!**

Do you believe that He is Lord? Do you believe that He has all right, power, and authority in heaven and on earth? If not, you need to repent and fling yourself on the mercy of God and beg Him to save you. If you do believe that He has all right, power, and authority in heaven and on earth, you must obey His commands. Rule #1: There is only ONE God. Rule #2: You are NOT Him!

The New Testament repeatedly confirms that Jesus was a Rabbi. He was openly recognized as such by all, including enemies and friends. In Hebrew, the word *Rabbi* means *teacher*. Essentially, there were two categories of Rabbis. There were the *Torah*

Teachers, and Scribes, who could only teach through reiteration of universally accepted truths. The other very limited group were described as Rabbis with *Smeka,* which means *authority.* This was a very limited group. They had the authority to teach new truths and give advanced interpretation of existing universally accepted truths. I cannot express how exclusive this group was. Josephus says that for at least 100 years, including the time of Jesus, this group of Rabbis with Smeka included less than 50 men! Rabbis were recognized as such because of having been discipled by a Rabbi. The more famous the Rabbi, the more prestige the Talmid. The title *Rabbi* was conferred upon ones performance in teaching.

Jesus was a Rabbi with Smeka is attested to by the gospels. Matthew 7:29 says, "For He taught them as one having authority, and not as the scribes." He displayed His authority over the spiritual realm when He commanded demons and they obeyed. He displayed His authority over the physical realm when He told the wind and the sea to be silent and they immediately obeyed His voice! It is no small thing when Jesus stood before His Disciples (of all generations) and declared, "All authority in heaven and earth is given to ME. Therefore, as you are going make disciples of all ethnic groups..."

The starting point of Making Disciples is not Making Disciples. The starting point of Making Disciples is the Lordship of Christ! *That's what we see here!*

Jesus said, "I am the Lord. All authority is given to Me! On the basis of *that* I want you Make Disciples of all nations! The starting point of *Making Disciples* is not Making Disciples. The starting point of *Making Disciples* is the Lordship of Jesus Christ!

Now with the "missions" emphasis that come to you in most evangelical churches on a regular basis, I'm sure that there are some professing Christians that are uncomfortable with that. They kind of check ahead a little bit and see that there's going to be another "missions" conference, or Pastor wants to lead you on outreach to the 'Hood, or to the County Prison, or to New Guinea, or China, or the African Continent. These folks think to themselves, "Oh no! Not another one of these missions things! Why can't we dispense with this missionary stuff and get back to church life as normal!"

I'm reminded of a man I once knew who didn't like Sunday. Did you ever meet anybody who didn't like Sunday? He'd say, "Round bout every Thursday, I feel Sunday comin on!"

This is the way some people feel about Jesus' command to Make Disciples of all nations, because its about your time, your money, your going, and your praying more. It seems that things like that kind of *bother* some people. And, *maybe* it bothers you, and you find, if you're really honest, a "resistance" in your heart to that kind of thing. You say, "Let's just get this thing over with and get back to Church life as normal." I just don't like this *missionary stuff.* If that's the case, if you honestly find a resistance and kind of an opposition in your heart to praying more, and to giving more, and studying more, to going more, and teaching more, your problem isn't *missions* nor *Making Disciples. Your problem is Lordship!* You see the starting point of *Making Disciples* is NOT these things. The starting point of *Making Disciples* is the *LORDSHIP of Christ!*

Neither God, nor the Christian life, is a democracy!

Neither God, nor the Christian life, is a democracy!

Now, with all due respect and deference to the American political system, *I'm here to declare that the Christian life is NOT a democracy.* It's not! We would like it to be, but it's not! The Christian life, as described in the pages of God's Word, is an "Absolute Monarchy" where there's ONE who is the KING, who gives commands to HIS subjects, and everyone who claims to be a

205

part of that kingdom OBEYS! That is a picture of the Christian life as given in the pages of scripture. The Christian life is NOT a democracy. It is governed by a Monarch!

Jesus Christ is Not a Constitutional Monarch.

You are familiar with the government of Great Britain, which is a *Constitutional Monarchy*. Great Britain has a Queen, a ruler, and her name is Queen Elizabeth. Question: Is Queen Elizabeth the person who runs that country? Answer: NO! It is a "Constitutional Monarchy". The people, by popular vote, elect members to Parliament. Then Parliament elects a Prime Minister to run the country. Today, in 2021, that man's name is Boris Johnson. He is the person who runs that country, NOT Queen Elizabeth.

In British Government, when Parliament decides to pass a law to tell the citizens what they can and cannot do, they always send the law to the Queen, in deference to her, with a dark solid line at the bottom on which they request she place her signature. In signing the dark solid line, she is, in effect, approving the law. But guess what? If she refuses to sign, *it's still a law!* Because she is a *Constitutional Monarch* and holds no real tangible authority over the governing of the country!

Jesus Christ is *not* a constitutional monarch, but a lot of people think He is! We get in our worship services and sing, "HE is Lord, HE is Lord! He is risen from the dead and HE is Lord!" We may even cry. But what we really mean is, *HE'S my king, but I'm HIS Prime Minister. I decide what I'm going to do. I decide where I'm going to go. But I would never think of doing any of those things without asking the Lord to come along and bless it all!"*

I meet people all the time who are making plans. And, as it were, they're writing their plans on a mental piece of paper - making a list. At the top of the paper, it says "MY LIFE." They put their name up there. Then, on that piece of paper, they write down all the things they are planning to do. They muse, "Well, I'm going to graduate from High School. I'm seriously thinking of going to Moody Bible College for a year. You know, get a little bible under my belt before I go to a "real" school, and get a "real" degree, so I can make "real" money. I mean after all, what're you going to do with a bible degree? That's not going to get you anywhere! So, a little bible, which would be good. Then I'm going to go to a "real" school, get a "real" degree, so I can get a "real" job. And, while I'm in school, I'm going to kind of look around, I won't be really obvious about this, but I'll look for a mate. You know a life partner. Moreover, I'm only going to be interested in Christians. I wouldn't want to marry a non-Christian. You know, the bible says not to do that. So, I'll only marry a Christian. Then, when we get married, and I get a job, we're going to find us a good church, like _____ Community Church, or _____ Baptist Church, or _____ Methodist Church, or _____ Presbyterian Church. And, we'll, within limits, get involved. You know, if they ask us to help in the Sunday school first grade class, we'll consider that. We might sing in the choir. And, we're going to give. Now, that giving thing is tough, but we're going to give. If there's a short-term mission's trip, maybe down to Peru or the Bahamas, we'll consider that."

> ## The greatest enemy of the *best* is NOT the worst, but the *good!!!*

Now, let me ask you, *did anything on the list I just mentioned sound wrong to you?* It all sounded good to me; perfectly legitimate. Remember this: The greatest enemy of the *best* is NOT the worst, but the *good!!!*

Next, they bring this list to the Lord with a dark solid line in the bottom right-hand corner. They'll bring this list to the Lord in prayer and say, "Lord, I'd like *you* to sign this page here approving everything that I'm planning to do." The Lord takes the page, looks at it, and says, *"Well, that's very interesting. In fact, really interesting, because I have a page that looks just like that that I was getting ready to give to you!* It's the same size as your page, and it's got your name on it. It's got a dark solid line at the bottom right-hand corner. See it there? And, this is what I, THE LORD, want you to do. And, I want YOU to sign down here, and when you sign, you're saying, "OK LORD. Whatever you say, I will obey".

You mentally look at the page, and you say, "There's just one thing Lord. The page is blank!"

HE says, "That's right."

"Lord, you mean that you want me to sign before I know what you're going to put on the page?"

HE says, "Yeah!"

"Well, Lord, my dad told me never to sign anything until after I've read it."

(Lord) "I just want YOU to sign!"

"Lord, can we talk before we get to this sign thing? What if you write on the paper…Mission field?"

(Lord) I JUST WANT YOU TO SIGN!" *"Lord, what if you write… Big City?"*

"I JUST WANT YOU TO SIGN!"

"Lord, what if you say…Africa?"

(Lord) "I JUST WANT YOU TO SIGN!"

"Lord, what if you say…Single, or …Poor…you know…no equity?"

(Lord) "I JUST WANT YOU TO SIGN!"

"Lord, what if you say...Martyrdom?" "I JUST WANT YOU TO SIGN!"

> **Jesus Christ is absolute Lord *of all* aspects of your life, or He is not Lord of your life *at all!***

Now, this is what I strongly encourage you to do. Mentally, get that blank piece of paper in your mind. If it helps you, physically write out your list! Next, ask yourself this question, *"Honestly, is there anything, that if the Lord wrote it on my page, I would not be able to sign; I just couldn't say Yes to that?"* Does anything come to mind? Maybe more than one thing comes to mind. If it does, then you have a *Lordship* problem! There is only one bigger problem in the sphere of Christianity. Romans 10:9, 10 says, "If you confess with your mouth Jesus as Lord, and believe in your heart that God raised Him from the dead, you shall be saved; for with the heart a person believes, resulting in righteousness, and with the mouth he confesses, resulting in salvation." In Greek, the English word *confess* is *homologeo*. It is a compound word. *Homo* means *same*. A *homogenous mixture* means the mixture is the *same* throughout. *Logeo* means *to speak*. The root is *logos*, which means *word*. It is also where we get our English word *logic* from. Accordingly, to *confess* means to *speak the same logic*. We would sum it up in the word *agree*. Confession is *agreeing with God*. The Bible is replete with passages extolling the absolute Lordship of Christ. In order to receive salvation, Romans 10:9 says that one *must* agree with God that, not only is Jesus the absolute Lord of the universe, but also the absolute Lord of your life! Jesus Christ is absolute Lord *of all* aspects of your life, or He is not Lord of your life *at all!* It logically follows that, if/since you have confessed Him as Lord, you must submit to His absolute Lordship and obey His commands.

The starting point of remembering our Lord and His command is not the taking of the communion elements! The starting point of remembering and obeying our Lord is His *absolute* Lordship!

You see, the issue is not *"Missions"* it's the *"Master."* It's not the *"Cause"* it's the *"KING!"*

> **Lord, the answer is Yes! Now what's the question?" That is complete submission to His absolute Lordship. That's the starting point of making Disciples of all nations!**

Some of you, who faithfully obey the Lord as best you (a fallen follower of Christ Jesus) can, need to go home today and take that mental piece of paper, representing your plan for your life, and tear it into a thousand pieces. Then, reach out, by faith, mentally, and take the blank piece of paper from the hand of the Lord and sign on the dark solid line at the bottom. In so doing you're saying, "Yes Lord, anyplace, anything, anytime! I'm ready! I'm willing! Lord, the answer is Yes! Now what's the question?" That is complete submission to His absolute Lordship. That's the starting point of making Disciples of all nations!

There's yet one statement in our mission statement in verse 20 that must be addressed. We don't want to leave out this part. This is the gravy. In this statement, the Lord promises to personally attend your ministry as you obey His command to make Disciples of all nations. He says, "Lo I am with you always, even to the end of the age." Now you can't see this in an English translation, but the word "I" is repeated in the Greek. It is the Greek way of "underlining". It would read, "...and surely, I – I will be with you...". "I" the Lord almighty will personally attend your ministry as you obey this command to the ends of the earth!

Tragically, just as the Great Commission is misidentified, many Christians rob verse 20 of it's context. They look at this verse and declare, "Well the Lord promised to always be with us Believers." While that is absolutely true, verse 20 is not a verse that makes that a blanket promise to *all* Christians. Other verses do that. This promise is specifically for those following His plan. This is a guilt-edge guarantee only for those following the Master's methods, pursuing His mission to the ends of the earth. This promise is only for reproducing Disciple Makers as they obey His mighty mandate!

I'm reminded of an event that happened in a small, rural, Kentucky church one Wednesday night. Before the weekly Bible study, the Pastor wanted to get the people thinking biblically. So, he asked that those who wished to do so stand and recite their favorite Bible verse. Several people did, and a big, strong, old farmer stood up and said, "Preacher, my favorite verse is 'go - lo…no go - no lo'." The Pastor said, "I'm not familiar with that verse." The farmer replied, "of course you are. Jesus said *'GO in to all the world and make disciples, and LO I am with you til the end of the age.'* You see the "Lo" follows the "Go". No "Go" – no "Lo".

Jesus said, "All authority in heaven and earth is given to Me. Therefore, GO…" The starting point of Making Disciples of all nations, and obeying the Lord is recognizing and submitting to His absolute Lordship!

> **This is not about *discipleship!* This is about *Lordship!***

This is not about *discipleship!* This is about *Lordship!* This is about Making Disciples in obedience to the absolute *Lordship of Jesus Christ.* Remember: It's not about the *cause;* it's about the King. It's not about the *mission;* it's about *obedience to the Master!*

Now go and make Disciples of all nations!

Footnotes

1. GTY.org, John MacArthur sermon <u>Preview of the Second Coming</u>

2. GTY.org, John MacArthur sermon <u>The Sufficiency of Scripture</u>

3. Shakespeare's <u>Julius Caesar, Act 3 Scene 1</u>

4. Truth & Life Ministries.org study entitled <u>Adoption</u>

5. From the book <u>Tally Ho The Fox, chapter 1, How Vital is Vision, Herb Hodges</u>

6. https://www.dictionary.com

7. <u>The Trinity</u> by Dr. Robert Morey, Christian Scholars Press

8. Confessions of Augustine by Augustine of Hippo, newly translated and edited by Albert C. Outler, Ph.D., D.D., Professor of Theology, Perkins School of Theology, Southern Methodist University, Dallas Texas, Database C, 2007 Wordsearch)

9. GTY.org John MacArthur sermon entitled <u>The Origin of Evil</u>

www.healthline.com >how many ribs do men have?

About the Author - Jim Douglas

Jim Douglas, born January 8, 1955 in Lebanon, KY, was educated at Taylor County High School, Georgia Technical University, the University of Kentucky at Louisville, State Technical University at Memphis. He is married to the former Amy Bachman. The Douglas family resides in Harrisburg, PA. Jim retired from the Department of Defense in Facilities Engineering.

For over 2 decades, Jim studied World Visionary, Reproductive Disciple Making under the mentorship of two pastors.

Combined, Pastor Roy A. (Soup) Campbell, Eikon Ministries, and the late Pastor Herbert Hodges Spiritual Life Ministries, both of Memphis, TN., have combined experience of over 80 years in gospel ministry and intentional, international, Disciple Making. Jim is a local, national, and international Bible Teacher, Disciple Maker, and speaker. For the past 30 years Jim has averaged 2-4 foreign trips per year leading short-term missions' teams abroad to train pastors and leaders on how to fulfill our Lord's Great Commission through World-Visionary, World-Impacting, Reproductive, Disciple

Making. He has partnered with such missions' organizations as Spiritual Life Ministries, Eikon Ministries, ProMissions of Memphis, Tn., and Global Missions Fellowship of Dallas, TX. He has taught bible conferences in more than 50 countries representing five continents in such places as India, Cambodia, France, Thailand, Philippine Islands, Trinidad, Jamaica, Venezuela, Mozambique, Mexico, Bahrain, South Korea, Honduras, Shri Lanka, Zambia, Botswana, Cameroon, South Africa, Kenya, and Uganda.

Jim is founder and Director of Truth & Life Ministries, which exists for the purpose of training world visionary, world impacting, reproducing, multiplying Disciple Makers, who will produce others in kind to the ends of the earth until the end of time. Locally and nationally, Jim teaches bible conferences, men's retreats, and conducts staff training at Christian Sports Camps. He trains small groups of men weekly. Over the past 30 years Jim has also been heavily involved in prison ministry in Dauphin, Cumberland, Lebanon, and Perry Counties, respectively, Pennsylvania. Jim is a member of Transcend Reformed Baptist Church in Harrisburg Pennsylvania.

Recommended Reading List

Tally Ho the Fox by Herb Hodges, Spiritual Life Ministries, Published by Manhattan Source, Inc.

Fox Fever by Herb Hodges, Spiritual Life Ministries, Published by Manhattan Source, Inc.

Fox Food by Herb Hodges, Spiritual Life Ministries, Published by Manhattan Source, Inc.

Disciples Are Made Not Born by Walter A. Henrichsen, Published by Scripture Press Publications Inc.

The Lost Art of Disciple Making by Leroy Eims, Zondervan

The Master Plan of Evangelism Revell Publishers

The Training of the Twelve A.B. Bruce, CreateSpace Independent Publishing Platform

Born To Reproduce by Dawson E. Trotman, NavPress

The Disciple-Making Pastor by Bill Hull, Baker Books

That The World May Know by Ray Vander Laan, Amazon

In The Dust of the Rabbi by Ray Vander Laan, Amazon

Twelve Ordinary Men by John MacArthur, Thomas Nelson Publishers

Twelve Extraordinary Women by John MacArthur, Thomas Nelson Publishers

In The Gap by David Bryant, Inter Varsity Press